Southern Legal Studies

SERIES EDITORS

Paul Finkelman, *Albany Law School*
Timothy S. Huebner, *Rhodes College*

ADVISORY BOARD

Alfred L. Brophy, *University of North Carolina School of Law*
Lonnie T. Brown Jr., *University of Georgia School of Law*
Laura F. Edwards, *Duke University*
James W. Ely Jr., *Vanderbilt University Law School*
Sally E. Hadden, *Western Michigan University*
Charles F. Hobson, *College of William & Mary*
Steven F. Lawson, Rutgers, *The State University of New Jersey*
Sanford V. Levinson, *University of Texas at Austin, School of Law*
Peter Wallenstein, *Virginia Polytechnic Institute and State University*

The Lost Translators
of 1808 and the
Birth of Civil Law
in Louisiana

The Lost Translators of 1808 and the Birth of Civil Law in Louisiana

Vernon Valentine Palmer

The University of Georgia Press
ATHENS

Paperback edition, 2024
Published by the University of Georgia Press
Athens, Georgia 30602
www.ugapress.org
© 2021 by Vernon Valentine Palmer
All rights reserved
Set in 11/14 Minion Pro by Kaelin Chappell Broaddus

Most University of Georgia Press titles are
available from popular e-book vendors.

Printed digitally

Library of Congress Cataloging-in-Publication Data

Names: Palmer, Vernon V., author.
Title: The lost translators of 1808 and the birth of civil law in Louisiana / Vernon Valentine Palmer.
Other titles: Lost translators of eighteen hundred and eight and the birth of civil law in Louisiana
Description: Athens, Georgia : The University of Georgia Press, [2021] | Series: Southern legal studies | Includes bibliographical references and index.
Identifiers: LCCN 2020041576 (print) | LCCN 2020041577 (ebook) | ISBN 9780820358338 (hardback) | ISBN 9780820358321 (ebook)
Subjects: LCSH: Civil law—Louisiana—History—19th century.
Classification: LCC KFL80 .P347 2021 (print) | LCC KFL80 (ebook) | DDC 340.5/609763—dc23
LC record available at https://lccn.loc.gov/2020041576
LC ebook record available at https://lccn.loc.gov/2020041577

Paperback ISBN 978-0-8203-6706-4

To my civil law students at Tulane—past, present, and future

CONTENTS

Acknowledgments — xi

INTRODUCTION — 1

CHAPTER ONE "All Rise. The Superior Court of the Territory of Orleans Is Now in Session" — 4

CHAPTER TWO The Hunt for the Lost Translators of 1808 — 12

CHAPTER THREE Henry Paul Nugent: The Story of a Mercurial Man — 20

CHAPTER FOUR Auguste Davezac de Castera: The Life of an Eloquent *Docteur* — 40

CHAPTER FIVE Reexamining and Exhuming a Pioneer Translation — 46

CODA — 81

APPENDIX Selected Writings of Henry Paul Nugent and Auguste Valentin Geneviève Davezac de Castera — 83

Notes — 101

Bibliography — 129

Index — 137

Illustrations follow page 45.

ACKNOWLEDGMENTS

I am deeply indebted to many colleagues and friends for their assistance, encouragement, support, and advice. First and foremost, I am grateful to Professor Olivier Moréteau of Louisiana State University, who, during the peer-review process, read the entire manuscript and gave me the benefit of his insights and suggestions. It was, coincidentally, his invitation to deliver the Tucker Lecture at LSU in 2011 that gave me the opportunity to delve into the history of Louisiana law in the territorial period and sparked my initial interest in finding out who the translators of the Digest of Orleans were.

I must generally thank all my colleagues at the Tulane Law School, particularly Dean David Meyer, for their unstinting support and remarkable patience in awaiting this much-delayed work. They may recall it was at our annual year-end faculty symposium some years ago that I made a presentation of my thesis and findings about the lost translators of 1808.

To Roy Sturgeon, Tulane Law School's gifted foreign, comparative, and international reference librarian, I am especially indebted. Roy was able to obtain for me a number of rare and obscure documents from remote holdings across the world, without which there would have been considerable gaps in the research. I must also thank Kristy Christiansen, media coordinator at the Tulane Law School, for her expert editing and help in converting the manuscript to the University of Georgia Press house style.

Finally, I wish to express my gratitude to the highly professional staff at the University of Georgia Press, particularly to acquisitions editor James Patrick Allen and his assistant Nate Holly, for the kindness and patience shown to the author and the close attention they gave to the publication of this book.

The Lost Translators
of 1808 and the
Birth of Civil Law
in Louisiana

INTRODUCTION

From a purely legal perspective, the first decade of the nineteenth century was perhaps the most fertile legal period in Louisiana history. After the transfer of Louisiana to the United States in 1803, it was necessary to build an entirely new legal system from the ground up. It was a period of prolific legislation, codification, and institution building. A territorial legislature was created, American-style courts were instituted, American judges were appointed, and jurisconsults were commissioned to draft the first codes. By far the most famous of these enactments was the 1808 Digest of Orleans, a civil code prepared by Louis Casimir Moreau-Lislet and James Brown. The digest was renowned as the first enactment of European civil law in the western hemisphere. It was indeed the first reception of the Code Napoléon outside of France. It was also a strong cultural statement by the ancient inhabitants of Louisiana of a desire to entrench their familiar French and Spanish laws rather than adopt the common law of the United States. A voluminous scholarly literature questions the circumstances of its drafting, the provenance of its provisions, and even why it was called a digest rather than a code.

The translation of this code or digest, however, has attracted little scholarly attention, even though in many ways it was nearly as important as the work of the jurisconsults. It was the first expression of a Romanist code in the English language; it provided the linguistic basis for the remarkable survival of civil law in Louisiana for the past two centuries; and it spawned an anglicized civilian vocabulary used by English-speaking civilians around the world.

The legislature called for the preparation of a bilingual code with French and English texts printed on facing pages. Both texts had the force of law, and the English translation was made "equally authoritative" with its French counterpart. Procedurally, the jurisconsults drafted in the French language and turned over their work to two men for translation. The legislature did not disclose the names of the translators, however, and these two individuals never came forward during their lifetime avowing their role. Thus the names, personalities, careers, and credentials of the translators, indeed everything about them, remained for more than two hundred years, until the present research, a missing chapter in Louisiana legal history. So little was known about the authors and circumstances of the translation that scholars have largely ignored their work except to criticize it for literal mistakes.

In writing this book, I had three principal aims in mind: to identify the lost translators, to explore and reconstruct their life stories, and finally to investigate and reevaluate their translation. As to the first aim, through archival research I discovered the lost translators of 1808 to be Henry Paul Nugent and Auguste Davezac de Castera. The opening chapter introduces both men in medias res on a critical day in their lives. The chapter is a true account of a dramatic trial when Nugent was charged with defaming a judge of the Superior Court, and his defense lawyer was none other than his cotranslator, Auguste Davezac. Chapter 2 leads the reader through the series of deductions by which their identities were discovered. It turns out that their names had always been in plain view, at least in plain *statutory* view!

Regarding the second aim, chapters 3 and 4 present the life stories of Nugent and Davezac in detail, or at least in as much detail as the historical record permits. Much of the information is new and was gathered from scattered and obscure sources. The chapters explore the men's sociopolitical connections and associations, their convergent and connected paths in New Orleans, and the credentials and experience they brought to the translation of the Digest of Orleans. The chapters also permit us to see Nugent's mercurial personality and sample Davezac's renowned eloquence.

Regarding my third aim, this book presents a fresh analysis of their translation. The analysis deals with Nugent's and Davezac's goals, the primary audience they held in mind, their innovations, misunderstandings, and the sociopolitical context of 1808. Furthermore, it attempts to bring the translation within the framework of the rich historiography of the digest so that insights gleaned from the translation may be applied to a number of debates and controversies. My overall conclusion is that the translation is a unique artifact of Louisiana's mixed legal system that mirrors the historical conditions of its day.

CHAPTER ONE

"All Rise. The Superior Court of the Territory of Orleans Is Now in Session"

June 12, 1810, New Orleans. The bells of St. Louis Cathedral rang ten o'clock. Close by, in a building called the Cabildo, the Superior Court of the Territory of Orleans was preparing to come to order. The small, rectangular courtroom known as the Sala Capitular was filled with a noisy crowd that had arrived early to find a place to sit. It was a throng of curiosity seekers, court regulars, legal grandees, and town notables, all speaking excitedly to one another in the idle moments before the arrival of the judge. They awaited the trial of a proud and petulant newcomer to New Orleans named Nugent who had written a pamphlet making sensational allegations about the character and behavior of a sitting magistrate. Nugent was arrested and indicted for defaming the Honorable Joshua Lewis, one of the three judges of the Superior Court. Judge François-Xavier Martin would preside over the trial.[1]

The trial was of immense interest to the local newspapers and lawyers because it involved judicial figures and raised fundamental issues concerning freedom of speech and of the press. Out in the first row of the gallery, with pad in hand, sat J. B. S. Thierry, the editor of *Le Courrier de la Louisiane*. A few days before, Thierry had been imprisoned for publishing an opinion about the case. He was found guilty of contempt of court simply because he published a piece commending Nugent's criticisms of Judge Lewis. Martin ruled that Thierry's article was "grossly and indecently abusive, and appeared to have been written for the purpose of making an improper impression on the public mind, in favor of a person against whom the Grand Jury had just found an indictment for a libel."[2] Nearby sat James Bradford, editor of the *Orleans Gazette*, quietly enjoying a moment of schadenfreude. He was thinking back to Nugent's satirical attacks, and he was not at all displeased to find his Irish nemesis in a legal quagmire.[3]

In the middle of the audience stood the distinguished lawyer, Edward Livingston, holding forth to a number of attorneys crowded around him. The small circle included Louis Moreau-Lislet, James Brown, and Étienne Mazureau, a veritable who's who of the territorial bar. They were all well aware of Nugent's contempt for lawyers. In a letter he published but did not sign, Nugent blasted the lawyers as so many plunderers of the people, with Livingston at the head of the "brigands." His dim respect for lawyers notwithstanding, Nugent had carefully chosen a talented team for his own defense. Heading his defense was Livingston's young protégé, Auguste Davezac, a lawyer known for his eloquence and ability to extract acquittals from juries, and assisting Davezac was Andrew Hunter Holmes, a young lawyer from Virginia.

Nugent was not without close personal friends and supporters in the courtroom. Julien Poydras and Pierre Dormenon of Pointe Coupée Parish had traveled the river by overnight boat to be on hand. Moreover, some of his students, girls barely in their teens, occupied an entire row in the gallery. They had walked to the Cabildo from their school in Nugent's home on Dauphine Street.

The courtroom chatter had practically raised to a fever pitch when the bailiff's voice suddenly brought silence: "All rise. The Superior Court of the Territory of Orleans is now in session, the Honorable F.-X. Martin presiding. God save this Honorable Court." A small, stoop-shouldered man dressed in black, with a large head and luminous eyes, entered by a side door and settled into a high-backed chair. Originally born in France and appointed to the Superior Court only months earlier, François-Xavier Martin was known for an iron will, a thin skin, and an encyclopedic command of the law. His translation of a French legal treatise brought him considerable cachet as a civilian scholar, and the recently launched law reports, which bore his name, promised to increase his fame and coffers.

The career of this highly intelligent and eccentric man, widely considered a miser, was destined to dominate Louisiana law and letters for the next four decades. Fiercely protective of his office and reputation, he wielded the contempt power and the libel laws to silence criticism and disrespect. He had already disbarred lawyers and imprisoned editors for the slightest insubordination, even for statements made out of court.[4] However, in his eyes the case before him went beyond mere disrespect or insubordination. To Martin, Nugent's attack on Judge Lewis was an attack on the judiciary and therefore on Martin himself.

Whether Martin could be fair-minded and should have presided at Nugent's trial were certainly open to question. It was not generally known, but Martin harbored an intense dislike for the defendant, and the ill will was mutual. It seems Nugent had written a damning review of the judge's signature achievement, his translation of Robert Joseph Pothier's treatise. The review called it a "contemptible translation" that succeeded in proving that "to translate Pothier, it is not necessary to understand the original, nor to have any idea of grammar."[5] Nugent threw in for good measure an unflattering assessment of Martin's ability to properly speak English and French. Martin's French, wrote Nugent, was more befitting of an Ostrogoth than a Frenchman. Not stopping there, he denounced the first volume of Martin's law reports as a "lying catch-penny."[6]

Martin had probably neither forgotten nor forgiven these stinging rebukes. Nugent's lawyers requested the honorable judge to recuse himself, but Martin peremptorily rejected the motion. He did not seem at all reluctant to try his most nettlesome critic.[7]

Martin motioned to his clerk: "Call the case of *Territory v. Nugent.*"[8]

A dark-haired figure in black waistcoat then rose and began to address the court: "Qu'il plaise à la Cour . . ." This was Auguste Davezac de Castera, a young lawyer often addressed on the street as "Le Docteur." The son of a planter from Saint-Domingue, he lost several brothers and the family fortune in the flames of the slave revolt. Reaching New Orleans in 1805, Auguste initially found work as a court interpreter. His sister Louise, who fled the island as well and reached New Orleans before him, married Edward Livingston, the most eminent lawyer in town.[9] Auguste served his apprenticeship in Livingston's office and gained admittance to the bar in 1808. His regard for Livingston bordered on idolatry, and Livingston now listened attentively to Davezac's opening statement.

Henry Paul Nugent, the man on trial, had acquired in a short time the reputation of an impulsive champion of free speech and a free press. His provocative and polemical writings, published at his own expense, tested the limits of press freedom in New Orleans, earning him a reputation somewhat similar to that of John Peter Zenger, the iconic New York printer whose famous trial helped establish truth as a defense to libel in the United States.[10] Born in Dublin and educated abroad in France and England, Nugent dressed well and carried himself gracefully. He was talented, versatile, and, by all accounts, a brilliant linguist. In his wandering life before settling down in New Orleans, he had performed in theaters as a dancer, opened dance academies, taught English, and translated French literary works. Arriving in New Orleans, he opened a school, worked as a translator, and became English editor of *Le Télégraphe*, a bilingual newspaper. He claimed to speak or understand as many as seven languages.[11]

Nugent still seethed over the indignities he experienced before the trial. The sheriff who arrested him called him an expletive (*gredin*, "dishonorable or disgraceful person") and threatened to assault him.[12] He was then held for several weeks in a miserable cell, unable to raise the very high bail set by Judge Martin. Furthermore, this was the second time that Nugent had been tried for libel and contempt of court. He was convicted at a first trial in 1807, but political friends and allies prevailed upon Governor William Charles Cole Claiborne to issue a pardon. Nugent did not yet realize it, but Judge Martin would contrive to have him charged a third time.

Nugent's pamphlet about Judge Lewis was the centerpiece of the prosecution's case. It was entitled "AN EXAMINATION of the opinion of Joshua Lewis, Esq. one of the judges of the superior court, . . . in the case of the Bayou Bridge.—Ecce iterum crispinus."[13] The title gave little hint of the rancor running through the pamphlet, for as any reader would soon discover, Nugent's objective was not so much to assess the merits of the Bayou Bridge case as to expose the "execrable conduct" of Judge Lewis in two earlier cases with which Nugent had intimate knowledge.[14] The author candidly stated his motives at the outset: "I with great alacrity, undertook to expose its [the Bayou Bridge decision's] absurdity, thinking this a fair opportunity to excite against Joshua Lewis that contempt and odium which he had abundantly deserved for his execrable conduct toward Mr. Workman and Mr. Dormenon." Nugent alleged that when Judge Lewis expelled James Workman, Esq., from the bar based on charges "not only frivolous, but utterly false," he acted with "nefarious depravity." After witnessing that trial, Nugent wrote, "I have ever believed him [Lewis] capable of all that is base and villanous [sic]."[15] Similarly, when Lewis presided over the disbarment of Judge Pierre Dormenon (the Pointe Coupée jurist accused of abetting the slave insurrection in Saint-Domingue some fifteen years earlier), the proceedings were so unfair that Joshua Lewis should no longer have been considered de jure a judge. Instead, he was in league with Dormenon's principal accusers, Louis Moreau-Lislet and Pierre Derbigny, to calumniate and scandalize Dormenon's reputation. In his reasons for judgment, Lewis stated: "It is considered that the safety of this country requires that no person who has acted in concert with the negroes and mulattoes of St. Domingo in destroying the whites, ought to hold any kind of office here, however fair their conduct may since have been."[16]

Nugent reserved his most explosive allegation for last.[17] He wrote that Judge Lewis had been observed by witnesses (one of whom happened to be Davezac, Nugent's lawyer) in the tavern La Fourche in a drunken debauch that lasted until 3:00 or 4:00 on the very morning that he was to try a man for his life![18]

The trial against Nugent progressed quickly and soon reached its close. Attorney General Philip Grymes placed Nugent's pamphlet into evidence, and the most damaging excerpts were read aloud to the jury. After that the territory simply rested its case. Nugent's legal team attempted to call witnesses to prove the truth of the assertions about Judge Lewis, but Martin refused to let the jury hear any testimony of the kind. He ruled that any testimony purporting to show the truth about Judge Lewis's judicial conduct or his alleged debauchery was inadmissible. Nugent was not allowed to put on witnesses to prove any of his assertions.[19]

Judge Martin then issued jury instructions concerning the crime of libel. Quoting William Blackstone nearly word for word, he stated that the truth of a writer's statements and proof of honorable intentions were *irrelevant* to the question of guilt or innocence for criminal libel. Yes, truth was a defense to *civil* libel, but according to Blackstone, it was not a defense to *criminal* libel.[20] Based on these instructions, the jury retired for only a few minutes and returned with a verdict of guilty. Nugent's sentence was ten days in prison and a fifty-dollar fine.

As soon as the foreman announced the verdict, Andrew Hunter Holmes for the defense rose and made a motion in arrest of judgment, contending that the grand jury's indictment of Nugent was fatally flawed and no conviction could be based upon it. The indictment, he argued, merely asserted that the libelous pamphlet had been published within the City of New Orleans, whereas it needed to state specifically that the offence was committed in the *first district* of the city, where the court had jurisdiction.

Somewhat surprised by this technical point, Judge Martin said that he would have to take the question under advisement. He therefore suspended the judgment for the time being and declared the proceedings adjourned. The court was now in recess.

A relieved Nugent walked to the rear of the courtroom, stopping to speak with a few students and friends along the way. He was temporarily free to go home, though of course the jury's verdict of guilty still hung above his head. As events were to play out, Martin kept the defense motion under advisement for the next seven months before finally declaring, in quite disappointed tones, that indeed the indictment was defective under English law, and the conviction could not stand.[21] Even then, however, the honorable judge was not ready to release the defendant. He immediately had Nugent rearrested on fresh charges, claiming that a more recent publication (published since the adjournment of the trial) called *The Greater the Truth, the Greater the Libel*, constituted a violation of the "good conduct" condition of his bail. Nugent was confined in prison for two more months until Abner Duncan, a New Orleans attorney, went security for his good behavior for another six months.[22]

The rearrest of Nugent was apparently Martin's best defense against the verbal onslaught he was receiving in the press. During the seven-month adjournment of the case, Nugent's pen had been on fire. From safe presses in Philadelphia and Natchez, Mississippi, he launched several broadsides against the judge that in length, sarcasm, and vitriol would be difficult to equal.[23] He also published a pamphlet from New Orleans in which he defended counselor Davezac's honor against "the calumnies of F. X. Martin" and pointed out errors in Martin's report of the trial.

The situation was inflamed: a trial that originally concerned the libel of Judge Lewis by Nugent had spiraled into an all-out attack on Judge Martin, who then ordered Nugent's rearrest. The behind-the-scenes insults and enmity between these men was certainly a sufficient basis for this war of words, but there may have been another factor hidden from view.

There was indeed an additional factor, never known before, that exacerbated the passions. The trial at the Cabildo in the summer of 1810 was not just an eventful day in the life of a powerful judge, his troublesome gadfly, and an up-and-coming lawyer. It was in fact a historic confrontation between three of the most influential figures in Louisiana law. These three men were in jealous competition not just as lawyers and press adversaries but also as legal translators, for unbeknownst to the general public and even all later historians, Nugent and his attorney, Davezac, were the incognito translators of the Digest of Orleans.[24] Two years earlier, in 1808, the two friends and allies had translated Louisiana's first civil code into English. The translation was a pioneer effort and a milestone in the annals of the civil law, for it was the first European-style civil code in history to be rendered in the English language. The impact on Louisiana's civil law (and on generations of English-speaking civilians to come) was far-reaching and significant, second only in impact to the work of the famous jurisconsults who prepared that code. The translation was a novel attempt, through the insertion of common-law terms and conceptual equivalents, to bridge the opposed legal cultures of bijural Louisiana.

This translation, however, was immediately declared, by a man who did not read or speak French and who did not understand the civil law, to be a failure. Governor Claiborne claimed it was an "extremely incorrect" translation, one executed by individuals unfamiliar with the English language and so defective that it might force the legislature to relinquish its goal of having a bilingual civil code. Interestingly, in his initial message to the public six months earlier, the governor had been far less critical. As George Dargo characterized the earlier assessment, "He [Claiborne] pointed to weaknesses in the English translation but was satisfied that no inconvenience would be caused by it." Now, however, his opinion had changed.[25]

The governor's reproach may have reflected the grim assessment of his advisors or perhaps influential members of the bar. Ostensibly, it was a powerful blow to the translators. It may have been one reason why Nugent and Davezac decided to downplay if not conceal their connection to the translation. Never during their lifetimes did they step forward to claim the honor or the responsibilities of translators. They kept their achievement to themselves. But it appears they did not act alone. A number of legal insiders seem to have been complicit in helping them maintain their secret, for their identity was not disclosed even by the inner circle of men closest to the codification project, namely, the jurisconsults Brown and

Moreau-Lislet and the house committee members charged with oversight of the project. The committee of oversight consisted of four members from the House of Representatives and two members from the Legislative Council.[26] Presumably, all these men actually knew and worked with the translators, but they also remained silent. The same complicity would have been true of various friends and confidants such as Julien Poydras, Edward Livingston, Jean Blanque, and others. They too said nothing, though surely they were well-informed and, in all likelihood, were instrumental in securing Nugent's and Davezac's appointments in the first place. Even the vilified judges who endured withering satire made no disclosure and did not attack the translation, though in their daily work they surely became acquainted with some of its deficiencies.

It follows that everything in the present work that now permits the identification of the translators of 1808 had to be gleaned from clues, deductions, and extrinsic corroboration, but never from the translators themselves or the avowals of contemporaries. Nevertheless, the research has lifted the veil of secrecy, and it will expose the circumstances of the birth of our civil law in the English language.

CHAPTER TWO

The Hunt for the Lost Translators of 1808

Lifting the Veil

The hunt for the lost translators takes us back more than two hundred years to the territorial statutes that announced the coming of the civil code. The earliest mention of the translators of the "civil code" (this was its common name not only before but even after it was promulgated as the "Digest" of Orleans) was found in a statute dated April 14, 1807.[1] It dealt with the subject of the compensation to be paid to the jurisconsults and the translators of the code. As to the translators, it provided that "a sum of seven hundred and fifty dollars . . . be allowed to each of the two translators appointed to translate the said civil code, the three fifths of which sum shall be paid immediately, and the remaining two fifths after the completion of the work, in full compensation for their services."[2] The act did not designate the translators by name, but it appears at least to acknowledge that they had already been selected, for it authorized payment of the initial installment "immediately." Assuming that they were appointed as of that date, then April 14, 1807, may be taken, roughly speaking, as the start of the translation. That beginning point fits well with the overall timeline of the project, for we know that substantial parts of the civil code were ready for translation by April 1807. The jurisconsults had begun drafting some ten months earlier, and Julien Poydras reported in January 1807 that the codifiers were "far advanced" in their work.[3] Thus, if April 1807 marked the start of the translation and March 31, 1808, marked its final enactment, then the translators completed their task in about one year.

Prior to final enactment, the digest received a "reading" in the legislature over the course of seven and a half sessions. In actual time, that meant an examination lasting merely nine hours. In Bernard Lafon's almanac (*Annuaire louisianais*, 1808) he drew attention to the undue haste, commenting that the brief examination would have afforded a citizen barely enough time to read through the code once. Lafon probably meant that it was barely enough time to read the digest in one language, not in both. A reading that attempted to compare the two versions for equivalence would have required weeks of study. Unsurprisingly, given such short legislative review, the digest was adopted "tel qu'il est" (as is), with not one amendment to the French or English text.[4]

Later on that same day, the legislature passed a second statute, which contains a direct lead to the translators' identity. This second statute set forth a list of persons to be paid for services rendered in connection with the "civil code."[5] The full title of the statute is worth setting forth: An Act Providing for the Payment of Sundry Expences Incurred in Revising and Copying the Civil Code. Eight names were then presented in the body of the text, and next to each name was an amount of money to be paid. We are not, however, told the precise service each person rendered: "Be it enacted . . . that the president of the committee for the revision of the civil code, be, and is hereby authorized to draw on the treasurer of this territory for the payment of the following sums: *to Augustus Davezac, two hundred and fifty dollars; to H. P. Nugent, two hundred and fifty dollars*; to Mr. Dupin, one hundred and twenty-five dollars; to Mr. Goudet, seventy dollars; to Mr. Missonnet, forty-two dollars; to Mr. Vassant, twenty-eight dollars; to Mr. Pomet, ten dollars; to Mr. Cuvillier, one hundred and seventy-five dollars."[6] It will now be shown that the two individuals at the head of this list—Henry Paul Nugent and Augustus Davezac—were the actual translators of the Digest of Orleans. Their link to the translation has been hidden in plain view (or, better, in plain *statutory* view) for more than two hundred years. True, the act nowhere states that they were the translators. It merely says that all the individuals on the list had performed services in relation to "the revision and copying of the civil code." But I will next present evidence to corroborate this conclusion. It will be shown by deduction, extrinsic evidence, and a process of elimination.

Coincidences and Probabilities

It is no coincidence that the companion statute referring to Nugent and Davezac was dated March 31, 1808. As already noted, that was the same day on which the digest was enacted and promulgated. It is also the one date that guarantees, without fear of contradiction, that the translation was finished. Since it is beyond dispute that the translation had to have been completed by the time the digest was enacted, that date was surely a logical and appropriate time to pay the translators for their services. It is not surprising that the legislature would put the expense of translation among the "sundry expences" incurred in "revising and copying the civil code," particularly when research confirms that there is no other statute or document, prior to or after March 31, 1808, in which the legislature purported to pay the remaining balance owed for the translation. The point, then, is that because we are dealing with a list of unexplained "sundry expences" being paid on the very date of the digest's enactment, there is already a reasonable probability that the translators' names would be found among the eight names listed.

Now further investigation confirms that the two names at the head of the list were at that moment professional translators working in New Orleans. The Irish-born Henry Paul Nugent was an educated linguist who immigrated to the United States in 1793 and took up residence in New Orleans in or around 1806. His native tongue was English, but he was sent to France for his early schooling, received a classical education in England, and wrote and spoke an erudite French. His publications display an extraordinary command of the French and English languages. He himself claimed that he spoke or understood as many as seven languages. The second individual, Auguste Davezac de Castera, was a Frenchman born into a distinguished and once-wealthy family from Saint-Domingue. He was educated at the elite Collège de la Flèche in France, and when the slave insurrection on the island killed some members of his family and destroyed the family fortune, he immigrated to the United States. He trained as a doctor in North Carolina and briefly practiced medicine in Virginia before immigrating to New Orleans. He arrived in New Orleans around 1805 to join family members already residing there, among whom was his sister Louise Davezac, who became the wife of Edward Livingston. His first language was French, but he wrote and spoke English fluently and, by all accounts, eloquently.

At the time when the digest was being prepared by jurisconsults Moreau-Lislet and Brown, Nugent and Davezac were engaged as sworn translators and interpreters attached to the Superior Court in New Orleans. This employment is verified by contemporary records and witnesses. In January 1808, some three months before the enactment of the digest, Governor William Claiborne reported to President Thomas Jefferson that "Davesac [sic] acts under the appointment of the Superior Court as Interpreter of the French language."[7] Vincent Nolte, a prominent merchant, stated in his reminiscences that he knew the Davezac family well, and he made particular mention of Auguste's work as a translator: "Davezac was of French origin, but had attained great readiness in the English language and was employed at the time of my own arrival as a sworn interpreter in the Courts."[8] Davezac continued as a court translator while concurrently apprenticing in Edward Livingston's law office. He was admitted to the bar in 1808.[9] He was later to become Livingston's law partner.[10] In 1815 he briefly reverted to the role of court translator when General Andrew Jackson was tried on charges of contempt of court for his arrest of Judge Dominick Hall and his decree of martial law just after the Battle of New Orleans.[11]

Nugent presented himself to the public as a translator and solicited work in that capacity. In several announcements, he reminded the public of his principal occupations: "I possessed no property, and depended for my support, on my daily exertions as a translator and teacher of languages."[12] Municipal records indicate that city officials regularly asked him to translate documents from French into English. When President Jefferson famously intervened in the heated controversy over the ownership of the batture alluvion, he called upon Mayor James Mather to send him a set of "batture-related papers." In filling the president's request, Mayor Mather commissioned Nugent to translate the entry "Isle" in J. N. Guyot's *Répertoire universel* and sent it off with other papers to the president.[13]

Nugent's career as a translator had begun in Philadelphia at least ten years before he arrived in New Orleans. There he translated various works in French, including *Collection of the Heroic & Civic Actions of the French Republicans*, which the *Aurora General Advertiser* ran in daily installments over a six-month period.[14] In 1815 he translated Arsène LaCarrière Latour's *Historical Memoir of the War in West Florida and Louisiana 1814–1815*, an account of the War of 1812. In 1808, during the disbarment proceeding brought against Judge Pierre Dormenon, when no one in the city was willing to come forward to defend the beleaguered jurist (Dormenon was accused of having incited slaves to insurrection in Saint-Domingue), "a translator" named Nugent came to his aid. He translated without charge the lengthy record of the proceedings into English as a public service to someone he thought was innocent and unjustly accused.[15]

Now reverting back to the significance of the names listed in the statute dated March 31, 1808, I submit that, given their occupations and talents as translators, the payment of $250 apiece to Nugent and Davezac represented, in all probability, the final installment of their compensation for the translation of the digest. Indeed, if for the sake of argument one were to claim they were *not* the translators, then it would be difficult to imagine what service they could have rendered that would have justified the payment of such a substantial sum.[16]

The probability that this is historical fact is strengthened by a process of elimination: it is clear that the remaining six persons on this statutory list could *not* have been the translators. These individuals had no vocation as translators, and in any event the sums they received were too small and incongruous to qualify as translation payments. These six men were all rather low-level governmental officials who apparently performed extra services that were related to their office.[17] If we recall that the statute dealing with compensation spoke of two translators and that each would receive the same amount, then those twin indicia—two individuals receiving the *same* payment—eliminate every person on the list from contention *except* Nugent and Davezac. Nugent and Davezac received an equal amount of money, the only two named individuals to do so. Their matching pay and their position at the head of the list (fittingly, the only names stated in full) suggest they performed some service jointly, as opposed to separate and discrete tasks. The other individuals received lesser and various amounts, ranging from merely $10 to $175. Those payments were not sizable enough to have been compensation for the translation of the digest.[18]

Two Convergent and Connected Worlds

Nugent's and Davezac's political and social connections in New Orleans were extensive and well-placed and would have facilitated their appointment to translate the digest. Each of them had ties to individuals close to the codification project, influential friends in the legislature, and connections with the leading lawyers of New Orleans. Their respective worlds tended to converge because they were close friends, often fought causes on the same side, and stood by one another in times of personal troubles.

The most valuable relationship for Auguste Davezac was with his brother-in-law, protector, and mentor, Edward Livingston. Davezac's devotion to Livingston was nearly total, and the affection was mutual.[19] Livingston's patronage could be counted upon whenever family advancement was concerned. Livingston advanced Davezac's career in various ways, for instance by providing the necessary law training in Livingston's office and by helping Davezac become the military aide of General Jackson during the War of 1812. Livingston's charisma and influence with judges, legislators, and codifiers could easily have accrued to Davezac's benefit. Certainly his warm relations with the two codifiers, James Brown and Louis Moreau-Lislet, could have afforded a direct means of advancing Davezac's name.[20] Codifiers are frequently granted the prerogative of choosing their translators (as Livingston himself exercised the prerogative when he chose Jules Davezac, his wife's uncle, to translate Livingston's penal code).[21] Moreau-Lislet had been the translator of Livingston's 1805 Practice Act, possibly on Livingston's recommendation. It is accordingly likely that Moreau-Lislet and Brown were in a strong position to request or to recommend the person(s) to translate their civil code and would have been willing to consider someone recommended by Livingston. James Brown was one of Livingston's personal lawyers in his litigation over the batture, and Brown once indicated he might have preferred to have Livingston as his co-codifier of the civil code.[22] According to Brown, the Legislative Council was originally of a mind to appoint a Brown/Livingston team to prepare both civil and criminal codes. Only Governor Claiborne's implacable opposition to Livingston led to Moreau-Lislet's appointment in his place. Brown referred to Claiborne's animus in a letter to Breckinridge: "The council appear disposed to engage Mr Livingston and myself to digest a Code; but such is the unfortunate dislike of the Governor towards the only man in whom the Council seems disposed to confide as my assistant, that it is believed the measure will fail."[23]

Livingston and Davezac forged strong alliances with other leading lawyers such as Lewis Kerr and James Workman. Kerr had personal and professional reasons to be receptive to the nomination of Davezac as translator. According to the governor, the threesome was an "unprincipled faction" and "very intimate." He described them as actively employed "in exciting opposition to the General and local Administrations."[24] Beyond having aligned political views, the men interacted in civic endeavors and sat together on various boards. Davezac and Kerr served on the board of the Library Society (Bibliothèque Société); Livingston, Kerr, and Brown were regents of the Collège d'Orléans.[25] It was also alleged that Kerr, Davezac, and Workman were fellow members of a secret society called the Mexican Association.[26] Claiborne regarded all of them as Burrites.[27] Kerr was arrested and charged in 1807 with setting Aaron Burr's plan in motion, and Livingston defended him in court, while Davezac issued press releases proclaiming Kerr's innocence. Workman too represented Livingston in the trial litigation over his ownership of the batture. This web of friendships and mutual interests should have enhanced Davezac's candidacy to translate the Digest of Orleans.

Nugent enjoyed the support of his Irish kinsmen Kerr and Workman, but he additionally had exceptionally prominent friends in the legislature. His connection to Julien Poydras, president of the Legislative Council and allegedly the richest Creole in Louisiana, was close and familial. Poydras was godfather to Nugent's daughter, Estelle, and was present for her baptism at Saint Louis Cathedral.[28] Poydras on several occasions served as an amical go-between for Nugent and was instrumental in settling some of his legal disputes.[29] When Pointe Coupée Parish established its public school system in 1818, Poydras invited Nugent to become the system's first headmaster. At the time of the translation of the digest, Poydras served as president of the Legislative Council. He was in a prime position to recommend Nugent's appointment.

Records reveal that Nugent had close relations with Jean Blanque, a wealthy member of the House of Representatives. Blanque served as Nugent's surety when he was incarcerated for criminal libel and contempt of court and was prepared to testify on his behalf at his trial. Nugent also became a friend of the codifier James Brown. Brown intervened as amicus curiae on Nugent's behalf when he was on trial for libel and contempt, and Nugent published a letter thanking Brown.

Perhaps the most significant indication of Nugent's connections and his standing in the community came in the form of a petition that circulated on his behalf after his first conviction for criminal libel. Signed by all members of the legislature, the petition urged Governor Claiborne to pardon Nugent. The governor issued the pardon in January 1808. This was six weeks before the digest was enacted, at a time when Nugent would have been putting the final touches to the translation. Characteristically, Nugent did not express gratitude to the governor for granting the pardon but reproached him for the delay in granting it.[30]

A Summary of the Historical Evidence

The discussion above constitutes the direct evidence for the identification of the translators. Let me summarize the main points. We begin with a list of eight persons being paid for "sundry" services in revising and copying the digest. The payment took place on the same day the code was enacted and promulgated. The two names heading this list (the only names stated in full) correspond to two professional translators then working in New Orleans. These translators received an equal amount of money (the only individuals on the list to receive an equal sum). It is the largest sum paid and the only sum commensurate with the amount promised to the translators by the legislature. All others on the list held unrelated occupations and received disparate and smaller payments, a circumstance eliminating the possibility that they could have been the translators. Furthermore, the names at the head of the list had extensive ties to the codifiers, James Brown and Louis Moreau-Lislet, and they enjoyed close links with prominent members of the legislature. Investigation of their social and political world suggests that their appointment was not a remote or illogical possibility but rather a plausible and feasible reality.

CHAPTER THREE

Henry Paul Nugent
The Story of a Mercurial Man

Nugent's Nomadic Life in the United States

From the moment the young Irishman stepped ashore in the United States in 1793, he began a nomadic and unplanned journey. He stayed constantly on the move, shuttling from city to city while keeping his eyes on no fewer than three or four possible career paths. At any given moment he presented himself as a translator, an interpreter, a professional dancer and dance teacher, an English teacher, a newspaper editor, and, at all times, a master polemicist. In later life, after settling down in Louisiana (1807–22), he became a professor of English at the Collège d'Orléans, and, shortly before he died, he was admitted to the Louisiana bar. His complete biographical details are rather difficult to assemble because official records are scant. Much of what follows has been gleaned from newspapers, random publications, and self-regarding comments interspersed in his writings.

Henry Paul Nugent was born in Dublin in 1772, and his parents were William and Ana Nugent.[1] He spent some part of his youth in France as a "schoolboy" and received a classical education in London and Bath.[2] According to one account, he graduated from the University of Dublin, but that information has not been corroborated and in fact seems rather improbable for several reasons.[3] First, Nugent was far from reluctant to brag about his learning, culture, and accomplishments, and it is difficult to believe he would not have mentioned his university education in his writings and advertisements. Second, since he operated a private school in New Orleans, it would have certainly burnished his credentials to make such a claim, and he himself never did. Third, Nugent's letter of recommendation from the mayor of Cork, written for him when he was twenty-one years old, stated that he had been living in Cork for the past five years. This chronology, his young age, and his residency away from Dublin would have made it very difficult to earn a degree from Dublin University.

In 1800 Nugent placed a revealing statement about himself in a Philadelphia newspaper in which he spoke of himself in the third person:

> He [Nugent] was regularly bred to letters and the ornamental arts, by which alone he has supported himself for several years. He was a pupil of Mr. Sheridan, the author of "The Art of Reading," and has taught the classics in a reputable academy near London. The art of dancing he learned in France and England, and he practiced as an assistant to the most eminent dancing master in Bath. The languages Nugent is acquainted with are the English, French, Latin, and Greek. These he has been accustomed to teach; but he wishes to teach the English language alone, as there are fewer skillful teachers of that language than of the others, as he has made it his principal study, and as the improvements which pupils make in their vernacular tongue, if properly instructed, render the task of the teacher no way irksome.[4]

From a work Nugent published in 1790, just before he immigrated to the United States, we learn that he had been teaching the English language at a private academy in Cork. Apparently, his views about proper English usage and pronunciation were already highly evolved, and he dared to criticize the pronunciation guide published by his own mentor, Thomas Sheridan. Just after Sheridan's death in 1788, Nugent published a new guide that bore the tendentious title *A Caution to Gentlemen Who Use Sheridan's Dictionary, to Which Are Added, for the Assistance of Foreigners and Natives, Select Rules for Pronouncing English with Precision and Elegance.*[5]

Nugent's life in the United States was at first frenetic because he moved frequently from city to city and from job to job. He often lodged in taverns and boardinghouses, where he had frequent encounters with other travelers and migrants. His movements would have been nearly impossible to follow had he not left a prodigious paper trail. The newspaper accounts reveal an irascible, proud, and excitable man who was constantly ensnarled in all sorts of controversies, often trivial ones with employers, landlords, innkeepers, and travelers he met along the way.

Despite a propensity to quarrel over trivial matters, Nugent must have had considerable charm and wit, since he managed to meet and befriend some of the most famous political and literary figures of the day. In New York he met Edmond-Charles Genêt, the French minister known for precipitating the infamous Citizen Genêt Affair. Writing in 1798, Nugent explained how his connection with Genêt came about: "[Nugent] happened to be employed as English teacher by some gentlemen lodging in the same house with Mr. Genet: Hence he became known to Mr. Genet, who offered him a salary as his translator, which Nugent accepted without the least scruple."[6]

In Philadelphia the following year, Nugent met Charles-Maurice de Talleyrand-Périgord, the powerful French diplomat, foreign minister, instigator of the Louisiana Purchase, and center of the infamous XYZ Affair. Talleyrand was then living out two years of exile in the United States.[7] Talleyrand reputedly spoke little or no English, and Nugent became his teacher and a friend.[8] A large community of French exiles lived in Philadelphia at the time, and Nugent frequented their circles. He was on intimate terms with the French minister to the United States, Pierre-Auguste Adet, and he also knew another French diplomat, Louis-André Pichon.

While living in Philadelphia Nugent performed as "principal dancer" at a local theater.[9] He also translated a number of French works, one of which, *Collection of the Heroic & Civic Actions of the French Republicans*, was serialized in a Philadelphia newspaper. He spent 1796 in Boston, where he also performed as a dancer at the theater. When the theater director dismissed him without cause, however, Nugent unburdened his grievances in the press.[10]

Nugent opened a dancing school in 1799 in Albany, New York, but a quarrel ensued about the leasing of the premises. Nugent suspected that he was being evicted in order to make way for a rival school headed by a man named Danglebert, who was supported by another Frenchman, Le-Couteulx. Nugent sensed a cabal forming against him ("cabal" being his recurrent word for real or fancied conspiracies), and he published his version of the *complot* in a newspaper. In the article, which was highly sarcastic in tone, he mocked the two Frenchmen in prose and poems. He said of Danglebert, who spoke little English, that "a cripple may with more propriety pretend to teach dancing than Mr. Danglebert, who cannot speak the language of his scholars."[11] LeCouteulx felt so insulted by one of Nugent's poems that he challenged Nugent to a duel. The poet haughtily declined the challenge, saying, "His claim to honorable satisfaction is inadmissible."[12] Then, in a deft shift to a safer subject, he challenged Danglebert to a dancing competition, in which, he vowed, the Frenchman would be outdanced.[13]

Leaving Albany, Nugent made a series of rapid moves in a southerly direction. He lived briefly in Annapolis, Maryland (1799), where he opened another dancing school, then Savannah, Georgia (1800), Charleston, South Carolina (1801), Washington, D.C. (1804), Lexington, Kentucky (1805), and Natchez, Mississippi (1806).[14] In Charleston he taught dancing and performed at the theater, holding at least one public performance for his own benefit.[15] In Lexington and Natchez he proposed opening schools, publicly stating his credentials as follows:

Mr. NUGENT,
HERETOFORE a principal dancer at the Theatre of Philadelphia, and Charleston, being respectfully recommended to this place from the City of Washington, where he taught last winter, purposes to commence a Dancing School in Mr. BRADLEY'S Ball Room.

Understanding that it is a general complaint, that the public are often imposed upon by persons professing themselves to be dancing masters, who are wholly unqualified for this occupation, which they have so vilified as to make it be thought the last refuge of imbecility; Mr. NUGENT thinks proper to lay before the public, the following certificate from the Revd. DOCTOR BUIST of Charleston,—sensible that the livelihood of a teacher depends much on the respectability of his character.

Charleston (S.C.) Oct. 29, 1803
Mr. H. P. Nugent was an assistant teacher in my academy nearly twelve months, in the year 1801, during which time he behaved with strict propriety and attention. From personal observation and experience, I believe him to be a correct and critical scholar in the English and Latin languages, and I have been informed by competent judges that Mr. Nugent is intimately acquainted with the French language, and is an accomplished teacher of dancing. At Mr. Nugent's desire I have given this certificate, which I consider as a debt due to merit.
"GEORGE BUIST"[16]

Wherever Nugent traveled, he continued to trade insults with actors, dancers, and travelers along the way. The pattern was recurrent: the translator was proud and thin-skinned, prone to take offense, quick to seek attention, and happy to publicize all disputes in witty press releases and bury his opponents in satire.

At last Nugent brought his considerable talents and mercurial personality to the Territory of Orleans, a new American possession since 1803 where English teachers were needed, dancing was popular, and sheer versatility might lead to gainful employment. In this new environment, Nugent underwent a change. He grew in maturity and stature. He engaged in public affairs, formed new friendships and alliances, challenged injustice in the courts, met and married his future wife, Josephina, and became the official translator of the Digest of Orleans.

A Short Digression:
Law, Language, and Translation in Early Louisiana

In the first decade of the nineteenth century, the New Orleans that Nugent encountered was a complex, cosmopolitan city. It was a small city by today's standards but a large city by American standards of the day. According to the census of 1806, the city had a total population of 17,001: 6,311 whites, 2,312 free people of color, and 8,378 slaves. Only five cities in the United States were larger at that time, and none was as ethnically or linguistically complex. The languages in New Orleans included Amerindian and African languages, Caribbean Creole, German, Spanish, French, and English, all routinely spoken by permanent residents. Richard Bailey has called it "the most compactly multilingual place in the country."[17] When the pioneering engineer and architect Benjamin Latrobe first visited the city, he was astonished by the exotic sounds around him: "On arrival in New Orleans in the morning, a sound more strange than any that is heard anywhere else in the world astonishes [a stranger]. It is a more incessant, loud, rapid, and various gabble of tongues of all tones than was ever heard at Babel."[18] French was by far the dominant language in the territory at the time of the Purchase. It was spoken by more than 90 percent of the white population and by many nonwhites as well, but different parts of the population spoke distinct varieties of French. Elite Creoles spoke so-called Plantation-Society French, also referred to as Colonial French.[19] The numbers who spoke this dialect greatly increased in the period 1792–1810, when boatloads of refugees fleeing Saint-Domingue reached New Orleans.[20] The largest wave reached New Orleans in 1809, when more than 9,000 arrived, consisting of 2,731 whites, 3,102 free persons of color, and 3,226 slaves. This more than doubled the French-speaking population of the city.

Plantation Society French served as the "high" or more prestigious language, ranking ahead of Cajun French, spoken by the Acadians who settled in rural Louisiana, and Creole French, spoken by slaves and some free people of color.[21] The literacy rate among whites was generally low, estimated as under 50 percent. This cannot be surprising, since at the time of the Purchase, Louisiana had no educational system at all. There were no public schools (other than a Spanish school conducted in Spanish), no public library, no colleges, and very few private schools outside of the well-known boarding school operated by the Ursuline nuns.[22] As Nugent himself observed in 1809, "There is not even a grammar school in the city, nor can a boy receive in this territory an education to qualify him for a learned profession."[23]

The anglophones in the territory initially were not numerous. They were generally native-born Americans who had migrated to Louisiana. They constituted only 13 percent of the white population (3,500 out of 26,069). However, if English at that time was only a limited medium of everyday discourse, still it possessed advantageous footholds that enabled it to become the prevailing language rather quickly. It was predominant in the conduct of government, in judicial proceedings, and in commerce. The strong link to commerce stemmed from the fact that "before 1803, being an American in New Orleans usually meant being a merchant, most often an agent of a large northern or British mercantile house."[24] Building upon these pillars and within a surprisingly short period (only a few decades), English supplanted French as the "high" language of Louisiana.[25] Apparently in the early 1800s the French language seemed too prevalent and well-entrenched for the Creoles to worry about the danger of its demise. To the contrary, their initial concern was that any consecration of French as the official language might jeopardize Louisiana's admission into the Union and the Creoles' opportunity to share the rights of citizenship with the rest of the American people. Therefore, the 1812 Constitution made English the official language of the state, referring to it as "the language in which the Constitution of the United States is written."[26]

At the same time, educated families were increasingly seeing the economic and social benefits of being bilingual, and this gave rise to a demand for private language academies, such as the school Nugent opened in his home. It was understood that to be successful in commerce one needed to know English, and English was thought to be "the main basis for the progression of the newly arrived."[27] One Creole youth observed that "without this language, it is impossible today to find a favorable position either in commerce or any other field."[28] Increasingly, the general citizen also grew more familiar with the English language. Nearly all the newspapers of this period, with the exception of *Le Moniteur de la Louisiane* (published 1794–1815), published bilingual editions and employed English-speaking editors like Nugent whose function was in part to translate news stories. The bilingual press included *Le Télégraphe, Le Courrier de la Louisiane, L'Echo du commerce, La Lanterne magique, L'Ami des lois,* and *La Gazette de la Louisiane.*

Lawyers had strong professional and economic reasons to speak English fluently, because throughout the territorial period, it was the official language of the constitution, of statutes, and of judicial records.[29] The Louisiana Constitution of 1812 designated it as the language in which all public records were to be preserved. As early as 1817 the Louisiana Supreme Court ordained that fluency in English was a prerequisite to the practice of law. The new requirement retroactively disenfranchised a number of francophone lawyers previously admitted. Equally significant, all the law books that the court set for aspiring applicants to the bar to read were in English or an English translation.

It is safe to assume, however, that any lawyer who knew English alone and nothing of French or Spanish labored under an impediment. He would have had difficulty attracting a first-class clientele and would have been unable effectively to communicate with all jurors and witnesses in the courtroom. An advertisement by two lawyers in 1804 called attention to their ability to converse with all clients, "let the language of the party be what it may," and emphasized their readiness to give assistance in French, English, and Spanish. Elite lawyers of the period, such as Livingston, Moreau-Lislet, Workman, and Mazureau, thrived in this complicated environment and enjoyed the most successful practices.

Under these circumstances, New Orleans had an inherent need for a multitude of translators such as Nugent and Davezac. Governmental offices, legislative halls, and courtroom proceedings could not function without the simultaneous or alternating use of two or three languages in daily operations. In his *History of Louisiana*, Martin painted a poignant picture of the complexities in a courtroom:

> Courts of Justice were furnished with interpreters of the French, Spanish and English languages. These translated the evidence and the charge of the court when necessary, but not the arguments of the counsel. The case was often opened in the English language, and then the jurymen who did not understand the counsel were indulged with leave to withdraw from the box into the gallery. The defense being in French, they were recalled, and the indulgence shown to them was enjoyed by their companions who were strangers to that language. All went together into the jury-room—each contending the argument he had listened to was conclusive, and they finally agreed on a verdict in the best manner they could.[30]

The practice of shifting languages back and forth in court was evident at Nugent's own trial in 1810. His jury consisted of six jurors with English surnames and six jurors with French surnames. Nugent mentioned in his account of the trial that "Mr. Davezac addressed the jury in French, and Mr. Holmes followed him in English."[31]

Nugent's and Davezac's arrival in New Orleans took place during the most fertile legislative period in Louisiana history. The territory was preparing to modernize its laws and in need of constructing from whole cloth a new legal system in two languages.[32] It would turn to a small coterie of lawyers and translators to build this bijural and bilingual system from the bottom up. The jurists behind the projects all came from the outside. All the jurisconsults and jurists (I include the translators in the latter category) were immigrants and/or refugees. Significantly, not one was a native-born Louisianian. All had received their education and legal training in another place or a different culture. Whether merely seeking fortune or fleeing revolutions, perhaps escaping from a collapsing world or simply hoping to find a better one, these "strangers in a strange land" were the first architects of Louisiana's mixed jurisdiction, though of course it was not called that then. The Practice Act by Edward Livingston, completed in 1805, gave the territory a small code of civil procedure known for its simplicity. It was drafted by Livingston in English and translated by Moreau-Lislet. The 1805 Crimes Act by James Workman abolished the archaic criminal laws of Spain (which condoned secret proceedings, cruel punishments, and use of torture) and substituted the English law of crimes. The Crimes Act was soon accompanied by Lewis Kerr's *Exposition of the Criminal Laws*, which Moreau-Lislet translated into French. The revised Black Code, the work of a legislative committee headed by the planter Étienne de Boré, repealed the previous French and Spanish slave laws and substituted more repressive laws using American models.

The centerpiece of this period was the 1808 Digest of Orleans, prepared in French by Louis Moreau-Lislet and James Brown. It was the first Romanist codification in the hemisphere, the first reception of the French civil Code outside of France, and, strangely enough, it was the only code in modern times to weave the law of slavery into its provisions.[33] Due to the existing sociological, linguistic, and cultural divides in Louisiana, however, the digest presented an additional challenge. The English translation would need to communicate effectively with a growing anglophone population that was utterly naive about civil law and culturally oriented toward the common law.

Nugent Arrives in New Orleans

Nugent arrived in late 1806 or perhaps early 1807 at the propitious moment when preparation of the civil code was already under way. He immediately sought means of earning a living. He opened up a language school, where, it was reported, English was taught to children of the "most respectable citizens."[34] But the instruction was apparently not exclusively for children nor restricted to the English language. It included adults, and other languages were taught. In one advertisement Nugent stated: "He continues to teach English, French, Spanish, Latin and Greek, Writing, Arithmetic, Geography, and the use of the Globes."[35]

Nugent pursued other opportunities besides running his school. He took on work as a sworn interpreter at the Superior Court, which no doubt introduced him to a broad cross section of the community. In this capacity, it is likely that he worked alongside Auguste Davezac, who held a comparable position. Nugent also accepted commissions to translate documents for the city administration. In the spring of 1807, merely three or four months after his arrival, he was appointed to translate the civil code.

Sometime in 1807 he also secured the position of English editor of the bilingual newspaper *Le Télégraphe*, a post that kept him abreast of public affairs, provided a podium for his political opinions, and made use of his talents as a translator.[36] On one occasion, he was called upon to translate from English to French an important speech in connection with the famous batture controversy. One reader (or perhaps the orator himself) complained that Nugent's French translation of the speech was misleading in that he used the French word *usurpation* to describe Edward Livingston's act of taking "possession" of the batture. The complaint argued that *usurpation* did not capture the orator's actual intent.[37] In answering the criticism, Nugent defended his work and stated his philosophy of translation.

> I do not take it upon me to translate the various acceptations of an author's meaning, nor, at all times, the meaning of the author himself: my task is to translate the meaning of the language.
>
> Davus sum, non Oedipus[38]

> Let the author say that I misinterpreted his meaning and I will acknowledge it, but it must be at the expense of his understanding. The obvious meaning of the word, the only one consistent with good sense, was as I rendered it.... That usurpation does in French mean wrongful possession of land, I have the authority of a respectable French lawyer in this city: "tout ce qu'il y a ... [word illegible] ou audela de 50 arpens est une usurpation." The Dictionary of the French language gives that word the same meaning. But though it had never been used in that sense before, it bears that meaning and no other in the case in question. In translation as in law, verba debent intelligi cum effectu, ut res magis valeat quam pereat—that is, words must bear a consistent meaning.[39] Usurpation in the answer bears no meaning analogous to the address, except the one I have given to it.... If anything else was meant, the answer is a Babelonian dialect:—one may say it alludes to the Inquisition, and another may contend it means only opposition to "being saddled with wooden shoes." Even if I had used the English word usurpation, the meaning would still be as I have more clearly expressed.
>
> In short, I am so confident of having faithfully translated the answer, that I am astonished to hear it denied by any who are not.[40]

Nugent did not shy away from taking a stand on either the batture controversy or other high-profile causes célèbres of the day. He worked to clear the names of (fellow Irishmen) Judge James Workman and attorney Lewis Kerr after General James Wilkinson, an American army commander, had them arrested as Burrites. Nugent also gallantly interceded on behalf of Judge Pierre Dormenon when the judge was attacked on all sides and threatened with disbarment. Nugent took considerable personal risk in denouncing Judge Joshua Lewis for alleged misconduct on the bench. His pamphlets brought him repeatedly into conflict with the judiciary and caused him to spend considerable time in detention. His writings frequently stirred heated reactions. For example, the editor of the *Orleans Gazette*, James Bradford, in a fiery piece entitled "More Treason!" called Nugent "a venal wretch, who is the automaton of a French faction in this country."[41] Nugent answered the insult with his usual asperity:

> Mr. Bradford,
> I hold your balderdash in too much contempt to notice it on my own account; but as your "more treason" may be read by men of intellects as deranged as those of the Senior Editor of the Orleans Gazette, lest any such lunatics should deceive men of plain understanding, my concern for us injured and oppressed people obliges me to expose the ravings of your insanity.[42]

Unsurprisingly, Nugent was a litigious man and made frequent use of the courts. A limited scan of the dockets of the Superior Court and city courts reveals that he filed as many as nine civil suits over a four-year period.[43] In 1821, the year before he died, he filed no fewer than six lawsuits.[44] Many of these suits were brought in propria persona. A lawyer once asked him why he did not practice law. Nugent replied, "My temper would not suffer me to acquiesce in the loss of a just cause: that . . . I would go to the utmost extremity to procure him [the client] satisfaction for the injustice that was done to him."[45] Perhaps his litigiousness was linked in part to a special sensitivity to injustice.

As a result of strongly held opinions and a penchant for ad hominem attacks, Nugent was arrested and tried three times for criminal libel. In each instance, the charges concerned intemperate statements about the territorial judges.[46] His first trial arose from a handbill that allegedly libeled Blaise Cenas, a justice of the peace. Nugent was convicted in early

1808 and received a sentence of two months in prison and a fine of fifty dollars.[47] At trial, the affidavit of Mayor James Mather stated that Cenas insulted Nugent while the latter was held in custody, and the provocation caused him to write the handbill.[48] A newspaper account maintained that the insult "tended to shew that he [Nugent] had received such provocation as justified, or at least excused, what he had published."[49] In these circumstances, his conviction was apparently perceived as a miscarriage of justice, and Governor Claiborne pardoned Nugent after receiving a petition urging clemency signed by all members of the legislature.[50] This unanimous backing suggests that Nugent had acquired a substantial number of supporters in the few months since his arrival in New Orleans. The timing of the pardon coincided closely with the completion of the digest. It came merely weeks before Nugent and Davezac submitted their translation to the legislature.

Nugent's writings testify to an extraordinary command of the English language. The weight of his words, including those that have been called his "code words," still makes a deep impression on readers two centuries later. Erica Johnson has argued that "perhaps it is appropriate that Nugent's biography remains a mystery, because his story might diminish the amazing power of his words. His employment of specifically chosen code words, such as septemberizing, drinkers of blood, black, tyrannical, and slave placed the story in greater contexts—the French Revolution, racism, the American Revolution, and the institution of slavery—and created a vivid illustration of the events and, more importantly, the significance of the trial. His use of language with great symbolic weight made his interpretation of Dormenon's case much more powerful, even more so than Dormenon's own account."[51]

Nugent's rhetorical references to freedom and slavery suggest that he was perhaps more liberal than his peers. After a trial in which he was denied the right to put on defense witnesses to prove the truth of what he had stated, he wrote in *Le Moniteur* that he had been treated no better than a slave:

> If in regard to my property, my liberty and my life I do not have the right to enjoy the blessings of liberty assured by the constitution, I am not free. It follows that I am a slave and all Louisianians are likewise slaves. Being a slave, . . . I admit that I deserve exemplary punishment for having dared re-

sist oppression and for putting on the airs of a free man. . . . I hope that my fellow slaves will learn from my fate to bend the knee before the three-tailed Bashaw and never dare to use the language of free men.[52]

Nugent's writings are dotted with rare and esoteric words (e.g., stercoraceous, flagitious, atrabilious, caitiff, oscitancy, Septembrisation). He also delighted in the elegant epigrams of Horace, Seneca, and Swift and the legal maxims of Lord Mansfield, Jean-Louis de Lolme, and William Blackstone. His pages were often embellished with Latin quotes that probably few of his readers understood.

His superiority complex about the use of language was unconcealed. It was evident in his disdainful and condescending critiques of other writers and speakers. Since he spoke and wrote English and French with exacting correctness, he judged others on the basis of their ability to do the same. In a sense, he weaponized correctness, mercilessly pointing out the errors and solecisms of others. He enjoyed mocking those who mispronounced words, or disregarded the rules of grammar, or pretended to have the skills of a translator. In lampooning an actor in Charleston, he once wrote:

> Whether your barking declamation, and your grinding of your words to powder (as a gentleman, speaking of you, well expressed it) be natural defects, and as such not to be objected to you, I leave to others to determine; but your ignorance of pronunciation and grammar admits of no excuse. *Drown*, you call *drownd*, and *drowned*, *drownded*; instead of pronouncing *door* like *more*, you pronounce it like *poor*. For *whither* go you? You say *whether* go you? If my recollection served me, I think I could fill a sheet of paper with the words and sentences that have been most tragically massacred by you on the stage, to my knowledge and that of many of the performers.[53]

Nugent's critique of Judge Martin's linguistic abilities was, to say the least, devastating. The insults he had heaped on Martin easily explain the deep animus that existed between them. The honorable judge, said Nugent, did not actually speak French or English but only a barbaric composite of the two. Martin's French, Nugent declared, "bespeaks rather an Ostrogoth than a Frenchman."[54] He recalled hearing certain remarks in court in which Martin used the French word *sollicitude* when he should have said *sollicitation* and when he deployed the word *déterrer* as if it meant to *deter*![55] The judge's translation of Pothier was actually a "contemptible" effort that proved that "to translate Pothier it is not necessary to understand the original, nor have any idea of grammar."[56] Nugent alluded to having written a "critical review" of the translation that probably Martin had read: "My critical review of his translation of Pothier, will, I am confident, convince such men as Mr. Gallatin and Mr. Duponceau, that there is a flaw in Mr. Martin's intellect. I have had many female pupils, just entering their teens, who could teach Mr. Martin either English or French grammar. But for proof of imbecility exhibited in his burlesque translation of Pothier, I should be surprised at Mr. Martin's venturing to give anything to the press, without having employed some person to put it into English or French."[57]

According to Nugent, this review was the real explanation for Martin's vengefulness in the courtroom. Regrettably for posterity, no copy of the "review" has been located, but assuming it to have existed, it would have been written sometime in 1807 or 1808, perhaps in connection with his research for the translation of the digest.

Nugent's Trial for Libel

Nugent's disdain for Martin's intelligence set the scene for their fateful clash in court in 1810, and it led to his fierce diatribes against Martin thereafter. The first broadside was a 124-page tract published in Philadelphia, a city believed distant enough from New Orleans to assure the safety of author and printer. The innocuous sound of the title—*An Account of the Proceedings Had in the Superior Court of the Territory of Orleans against Thierry and Nugent for Libels and Contempt of Court, with an Account of Nugent's Trial on an Indictment for a Libel*—disguised its angry purpose. At the foot of the first page was written, "Printed for the Use of the Members of Congress, and of the Orleans Legislature." If anyone thought that this would be an unbiased "account" of the trials, however, he or she was quickly disabused. It was essentially a platform for satire, sarcasm, and revenge.

A second attack came in 1811. This was *H. P. Nugent's Reply to the Calumnies of the Honorable F. X. Martin, One of the Judges of the Superior Court of the Territory of Orleans*. According to the author, all printers in New Orleans declined to print it because they lived in "dread of the lawless rage of the honorable F. X. Martin." The author was forced to apply outside the territory "to a printer living beyond the reach of tyranny."[58] Nugent found that printer in Natchez.

As an opening salvo Nugent decried the national calamity of having "dolts" such as Martin and Lewis on the bench. He sarcastically invited Martin to enroll in his school to learn the rules of grammar.[59] He then dredged up reams of demeaning gossip about the eccentric jurist.[60] Reference was made to Martin's lechery and "libidinous amours," which then became a string of adjectives: "the lecherous, treacherous, bloody, bawdy villain." Martin's relentless pursuit of wealth ("the vice of avarice has taken deep root in his soul") was a prime subject: "He loves money more than he dreads infamy." According to Michael Chiorazzi, Martin's estimated wealth on his arrival in Louisiana was $100,000. As a judge he received a salary of $2,000 per year. His estate at death was valued at $400,000, which in current money might be the equivalent of nearly $8 million.[61]

The satire next took the guise of absurd dispatches appearing in the *Ispahan Gazette* in Persia, the same gazette reporting in Montesquieu's *Lettres persanes*. One dispatch brought news of a hapless Persian lawyer named "Mirtan" whom the emperor had raised to the dignity of cadi, or Muslim judge who administers Islamic law. No detail was spared in describing the cadi's grotesque appearance: "Never indeed was cast in the mould of nature a more sorry abortion of humanity.... A grinning aspect, a tottering gait, a stupid look, a ragamuffin garb, all of him that strikes the eye, would, in any large city, make him be taken for a sow-gelder, or a hawker of old cast clothes." The cadi, blithely ignorant of his deficiencies, thought he was an accomplished translator and musician. His translation of Confucius into Persian led to "ruining his bookseller, and of being hissed for his numberless solecisms, barbarisms and blunders." The translator "possesses the gift of tongues by intuition, except however that of his own." As a musician he played incessantly an instrument called the "Houhou." His progress was so plodding that "in somewhat less than six months, by practicing 6 hours a day, he has almost half learned his favorite air. In vain does his melody set the cocks a crowing, the dogs a barking, the cats a caterwauling, and the neighbours a cursing."[62]

This parody could make one forget that there was a substantive point behind it. Nugent's underlying claim was that the courts and judges of the day were overstepping all bounds and using the law of contempt and libel as an instrument of oppression. His personal experiences in court led him to conclude that the judges were a threat to constitutional liberties. He compared the oppression of the judges to the excesses and crimes of the French Revolution: "It seems then that our judges have erected their court into a committee of public safety, and in imitation of Robespierre and his accomplices, endeavor to strengthen the arm of government, by establishing a system of terror, and destroying the liberty of the press."[63] His courageous defense of others and his refusal to be silenced have been compared to John Peter Zenger's defense of press freedom.[64] He reveled in an aphorism that became a personal motto: "While truth is a libel, I glory in the title of libeler."

Nugent's Marriage to Josephine Ruotte

In 1812 Nugent married into the distinguished Ruotte family. His wife, Josephine (*née* Maria Catarina Josephine Ruotte), was born at Cap-Français, the daughter of Antoine-Étienne Ruotte and Anna Beck.[65] Anna Beck was a native of Belfast, Ireland, and thus Josephine was half-Irish and half-French. Probably she grew up in a bilingual household and spoke English and French fluently. That ability no doubt made her an invaluable partner in running Nugent's language school in New Orleans. Josephine's father was a Creole born in Martinique (or Guadeloupe, as some sources say) into a family originally from Toulouse. Antoine was a planter, a decorated official, and one of the island intellectuals who founded the Cercle des Philadelphes, a scientific society in Saint-Domingue.[66] Probably he held a law degree from the University of Toulouse, for in Saint-Domingue he had held the positions of *substitut du procureur* (deputy prosecutor) and *subdélégue de l'intendant* (deputy intendant). He served for nearly two decades (1770–88) as a *conseiller* (magistrate or judge) on the Conseil superièure of Cap-Français. In the course of time he earned the title *conseiller titulaire* (titular advisor), as well as the title *doyen* (dean) of the council.[67] It has not been determined where or when Antoine-Étienne died, but it is clear that he did not come to New Orleans. According to his son, he was deported to New England and died there, but no date or details were given. Historian Médéric Louis Élie Moreau de Saint-Méry relates that the Ruotte family possessed considerable wealth—a coffee plantation at Petite-Anse on Saint-Domingue, and several homes at Cap-

Français—but this "brilliant fortune" was all lost in the slave revolt.[68] Josephine, along with her mother, Anna, and her sister, Marguerite, fled the island and arrived in New Orleans sometime in 1805. They brought a certain number of slaves with them, two of which Anna promptly sold in order to raise cash.[69]

Nugent was forty years old and Josephine merely nineteen at the time of their marriage. As Eberhard Faber points out, intermarriages such as theirs between Creoles and Americans were "fairly common" in early Louisiana.[70] They soon had two daughters, Henriette, born in 1815, and Estelle Julienne, born in 1817.

Somewhat less is known of Nugent's life after his marriage to Josephine. It is clear that he continued to operate a school where he taught "English, French, Spanish, Latin and Greek, Writing, Arithmetic, Geography, and the use of the Globes."[71] In 1814 he accepted the position of "Professor in the English Language" at the Collège d'Orléans. Within a short while he resigned the position, apparently because his salary was reduced and he found the faculty regulations burdensome.[72] The next step is not certain, but sometime in 1815 the Nugents may have left Louisiana briefly and relocated in Albany, New York. An advertisement in the *Albany Gazette* invited women and men students to take classes in a school jointly run by Mr. and Mrs. Nugent, but if this was in fact a reference to the Nugents from New Orleans, then the venture did not materialize or was abandoned quickly.[73] By 1816 Nugent was certainly living and working in New Orleans, where, in his inimitable style, he publicly denounced a rival school using the Lancasterian method of instruction. He roundly castigated "these shameless impostors calling themselves Lancastrian teachers, whose imbecility would sink them below the notice of any respectable school master."[74]

Around 1815 Nugent accepted a commission to translate Arsène LaCarrière Latour's *Historical Memoir of the War in West Florida and Louisiana, 1814–1815*, which was published in Philadelphia. Originally written in French, the book totaled 491 pages in length, including an atlas and appendix containing more than one hundred documents. Latour was a French architect and civil engineer who came to New Orleans in 1806. General Jackson appointed him principal engineer for the Seventh Military District of the US Army. In that capacity, he laid out the defensive works for the Battle of New Orleans and was present during the fighting.

His memoir relied on primary documents and eye-witness accounts and became a definitive account of Jackson's campaign. As to the quality of Nugent's translation, one reviewer stated: "Latour wrote in a clear, direct style and the original English translation is relatively transparent, with the result that the text flows well."⁷⁵

Nugent's Second Clash with the Regents

In 1818 Nugent accepted reappointment as professor of the English language at the Collège d'Orléans. This was apparently the same position that he had resigned from four years before. Once again, his employment was brief and ended contentiously. Apparently, Nugent regarded the regents' new faculty regulations as intolerable. One regulation required the professors of French and English to teach courses in history and geography in addition to their principal subjects and to compose lesson summaries for the students. The teacher was to create "analytical abstracts of such parts of those Sciences [history and geography] as are to be made the object of these lessons, and to dictate the same to their said students who shall copy them on a stitched book for immediate use."⁷⁶ To Nugent, the regulation was condescending—more befitting of a grammar school than of a college. Stuart Grayson Noble has pointed out, however, that the Collège d'Orléans was indeed little more than a grammar school: "The College of New Orleans, in the fifteen years of its career, never rose to the rank of a college as we understand the word today. Its course of study even in its day was never regarded as of collegiate grade. . . . [T]he College of New Orleans opened its doors as a grammar school of the type then familiar in Europe and in the Atlantic states. As such it entered into active competition with private schools of the same rank."⁷⁷

The second regulation was obnoxious to a professor like Nugent, who operated a private school of his own. It forbade the professors to give private courses outside of the college.⁷⁸ Obviously, if he complied with the regulation, he would have been obliged to close his school. Nugent did not quietly circumvent or flout these regulations. He attacked them publicly. In a witty piece entitled "Gulliver's Account of the Grand Academy of Projectors at Lagado," he mocked the regulations and denounced the regents. His piece concludes with the declaration: "The Regents do me too much honor in taking me for a universal genius. I will therefore continue

38 CHAPTER THREE

to teach as I was taught myself." Below his signature he listed his titles and added a final riposte: "H. P. Nugent, Professor of English, in the Collège d'Orléans, and Teacher of English, French, Spanish, Latin and Greek at his own house, in contempt and derision of the imperial decree by which a pragmatical French cabal falsely calling themselves the Board of Regents forbids Professors to teach out of the College."[79]

The unamused regents regarded the publication as "scurrilous and abusive" and more than sufficient reason for Nugent's discharge, which they carried out immediately.[80] But in the haste to dismiss Nugent, the regents failed to afford him a hearing and thus failed to follow the elementary rule audi alteram partem, or "hear the other side." Nugent sued for reinstatement, and the case came before Judge Joshua Lewis. No doubt to the translator's immense satisfaction, the judge whom Nugent once called a "national calamity" and a "dolt" ruled in his favor. Judge Lewis held that Nugent's dismissal without a hearing violated a fundamental rule of natural justice, and he issued a writ of mandamus ordering reinstatement. The regents appealed the decision to the state supreme court.[81]

A Fresh Start in Pointe Coupée

After his dismissal by the regents, Nugent moved his family to Pointe Coupée, a small community some fifty miles upriver from New Orleans.[82] He accepted an offer extended by Julien Poydras and Pierre Dormenon on behalf of the school board to become headmaster of the newly created Pointe Coupée Public School.[83] Under the terms of his contract, the parish would provide him a home at public expense and a salary of $2,400 per year (in return for boarding and educating twelve scholars), and the state would supplement his salary by $600 per year.[84]

Sometime in 1822 Nugent filed a complaint with the Louisiana Senate charging Pointe Coupée parish judge Louis Esneault with judicial misconduct.[85] The complainant asked the Senate to conduct an investigation. Nothing is known of the substance of the charge or the outcome of the investigation, yet it shows that Nugent's relations with the judiciary remained as tempestuous as ever.[86]

Also in 1822 Nugent sought to collect a debt from Louis Roland for room and board. The defendant counterclaimed for a greater sum than Nugent sought, and the jury returned a verdict for the defendant. Nugent's appeal from that decision to the state supreme court brought together his friends and foes. James Workman represented Nugent, Auguste Davezac represented Roland, and the Honorable François-Xavier Martin, wrote the court's opinion.[87] In a ruling pronounced after Nugent's death, the court held in Roland's favor.

Nugent's final lawsuit before his death was against the Pointe Coupée Parish School Board for breach of contract and fraud. By the vehement tone of the petition it is clear that relations with the board had broken beyond all repair. Apparently when Julien Poydras stepped down as president of the school board and Dr. Auguste Provosty took over in his place, the board's policies and generous feelings toward Nugent also changed.[88] According to the petition, the legislature had increased the headmaster's salary supplement from $600 to $800, yet the board "fraudulently" refused to pay the plaintiff the increased sum. Nugent sued not only to recover this sum but also for pain and suffering brought about by the board's "fraud." In laying personal claim to the salary supplement, Nugent declared that he was "the only school master legally qualified, in this parish, to receive public money . . . the only school master in the parish who understood such [classical Greek and Latin] books . . . the only school master in the parish who knew the English Language; and that therefore the petitioner had a right to the whole sum of eight hundred Dollars." Judge Esneault, however, dismissed the suit and taxed Nugent with costs.[89]

Nugent passed away on August 22, 1822, in Pointe Coupée at the age of fifty.[90] The cause of death is unknown, but apparently he had been in bad health for some time. A witness who visited his home a few months earlier found him ill and confined to bed.[91]

Five years later his widow, Josephine, married Jean Olere (perhaps spelled O'Leary), with Judge Pierre Dormenon as her witness.[92] Josephine lived only one year longer, leaving the two Nugent daughters as orphans.

In 1821, one year before his death, Nugent became a member of the bar.[93] There was obviously little or no time to establish a law practice. His name has not been located as counsel of record in any reported appellate case.[94]

CHAPTER 4

Auguste Davezac de Castera
The Life of an Eloquent *Docteur*

Auguste Davezac came from a prominent family in Saint-Domingue that possessed indigo, coffee, and sugar plantations. He was born at Aux Cayes in May 1781, the third son of Jean Pierre Valentin Joseph D'Avezac de Castera and Marie Rose Geneviève Valentine de Maragou. The plantation had an extensive library, and Auguste was educated by private tutors, then sent for studies in France at the military college of La Flèche. After two brothers and his grandmother were killed during the slave rebellion, he immigrated to the United States and studied medicine in Edenton, North Carolina. During this period he modified the spelling of his name from D'Avezac to Davezac simply by eliminating the apostrophe.[1] On completing his studies, he opened a medical practice in Virginia and married Margaret Andrews, who was twelve years his senior.[2] Their child, Auguste Davezac Jr., was born shortly before the family moved to New Orleans in 1805 or 1806.[3] The move enabled Auguste to join other members of his family—his mother, his two sisters, Aglaé and Louise, and his uncle Jules—who had taken refuge in the city a short time before.[4] In June 1805 his sister Louise married Edward Livingston. Abandoning his budding career in medicine, Davezac took up the study of law under Livingston's guidance. Even after he was admitted to the practice of law, he continued to be addressed in New Orleans society as "Le Docteur Davezac."[5]

Auguste's aptitude for languages gained him immediate employment as a sworn interpreter attached to the courts. The cotton merchant Vincente Nolte, in sketching the Livingston-Davezac family in his reminiscences, made mention of Davezac's work and of his close ties to Livingston:

The lady's maiden name had been Davezac, and, after the destruction of the colony [Saint-Domingue], she had fled with her mother, sister, and one brother, first to Jamaica, and then to Louisiana. I shall hereafter find further occasion to speak of Livingston's brother-in-law, Auguste Davezac. He was the same person who, some years after, was appointed by President Jackson to the post of American Ambassador, and was from there summoned to Naples to draw the indemnity moneys, but was soon after obliged to give up his place at the Hague, on account of what we will call—to use a mild term—irregularities in the arrangements of his accounts. Davezac was of French origin, but had attained great readiness in the English language and was employed at the time of my own arrival as a sworn interpreter in the Courts, and he was afterwards in the Legislative Assembly of Louisiana. He had at length become Livingston's factotum, and had made himself almost indispensable to that gentleman, in hunting up the evidence among the family papers of the French planters, and in procuring witnesses who were ready at all times to swear to anything that might be required of them.[6]

Certain historians have apparently confused Auguste with his uncle Jules Davezac, a learned older gentleman living full-time in the Livingston household. One account has it that Jules practiced law and was Livingston's brother-in-law, but this is simply a case of mistaken identity. Jules (Pierre Galentin Dominique Julian D'Avezac) was a man of letters, the first president of the Collège d'Orléans, and a distinguished translator and poet in his own right.[7] He was neither a lawyer nor Livingston's brother-in-law.[8] He served as secretary and recorder in the New Orleans mayor's office during the Roffignac administration from 1820 to 1828.[9] Though he could read and understand English, he did not speak a word of it. Livingston called upon Jules to produce the French translation of his famous penal code (the text was drafted in English), and the exceptional quality of the translation has been said to be partly responsible for the great reputation that the code enjoyed on the Continent.[10] Commenting on Jules Davezac's translation of the Livingston penal code, Charles Havens Hunt noted:

> In this work the translator evinced a singularly exact comprehension of his author's meaning even to minute and technical particulars. What made this very remarkable was the fact that M. Davezac had acquired the English as one acquires a dead language, was entirely unacquainted with its sounds, and never learned to comprehend the simplest conversation in that tongue. It was chiefly through this version that the Code . . . became known on the

continent of Europe. The French critics commended the general purity of its style, and pointed out only three or four instances of what they might have termed "Americanisms." . . . With these reservations the composition was pronounced to be a marvel for a production coming from the Western wilderness.[11]

Incidentally, there was another gifted translator and lawyer in the family, and this was Henry Carleton, who married Auguste's sister Aglaé and later on, along with Louis Moreau-Lislet, translated *Las siete partidas* into English.

Legal Training and Practice

Auguste apprenticed in Livingston's law office for several years, and they became close friends and political allies for life.[12] An apprenticeship for at least three years was necessary for admission to practice before the Superior Court, and Auguste made his first appearance as a lawyer in 1808. In his first year of practice, he was briefly disbarred by Judge Joshua Lewis but was shortly thereafter reinstated.[13] In the summer of 1810, he was defense counsel for Henry Paul Nugent in his trial for the criminal libel of Judge Lewis.[14] When Louisiana reached statehood, Davezac was among the first lawyers to enroll before the newly created Louisiana Supreme Court, which convened on March 2, 1813.[15]

In his private practice, Davezac specialized in criminal defense work, and from time to time he represented Baratarian privateers and smugglers in the courts. According to Janet Deitch Young, "He took no pains to hide his friendship with the pirate brothers, Jean and Pierre Lafitte, walking arm and arm with them on the street and acting as their lawyer in the sale of slaves and the exchange of deeds at the Maspere Bank."[16] Nolte also mentioned Lafitte and other celebrated pirates parading arm in arm in the streets of New Orleans with Davezac, whom they regarded as a "bosom-friend." The pirates were caught several times, but according to Nolte, Livingston and Davezac always managed to get them released.[17]

Davezac was particularly known for his eloquence in court and was considered without peer as a criminal lawyer. No client of his ever suffered the death penalty.[18] He was constantly retained in homicide cases and, according to one source, had an extensive if not first-class clientele.[19] His civil practice, though probably smaller than his criminal practice, was certainly not insubstantial. Martin's law reports record at least twenty-four civil cases that Davezac argued before the Superior Court and the Supreme Court of Louisiana.[20]

During the War of 1812 Davezac served along with Livingston on the local Committee for Public Safety, and at the time of the battle of New Orleans in 1815 he served as General Jackson's aide-de-camp with the rank of major.

Davezac's Political Career with Edward Livingston and Andrew Jackson

In 1816 Davezac was elected to the state House of Representatives, representing Rapides Parish.[21] In 1820 he was elected to the state House representing New Orleans, and in the same election Livingston secured a seat in the U.S. Congress. In 1822 Davezac and Livingston ran together on the same ticket and were reelected. That same year, Livingston, Pierre Derbigny, and Louis Moreau-Lislet were selected to be jurisconsults to prepare a new civil code, as well as new codes of commerce and procedure. Conveniently, Davezac was chairman of the code revision committee in the House and gave unqualified backing to these projects. In his committee's report approving the plans of the jurisconsults, Davezac wrote: "The sketch they have given affords a favorable presage of the skill with which the work will be executed: The hands which have marked the outlines with so much boldness, cannot fail in the details."[22] He also supported Livingston's efforts to codify a criminal code.

Andrew Jackson was a heroic figure to Davezac, and he threw himself into the general's 1828 campaign for president. As he later explained to Ralph Waldo Emerson, "He [Jackson] became my destiny! I instinctively foresaw his greatness and glory. My attachment to him was a religion of the heart!"[23] Jackson rewarded Davezac's loyalty with the diplomatic post of secretary to the U.S. Embassy in the Netherlands, where he served as chargé d'affaires from 1831 to 1839. On his return from the Netherlands, he moved his residence from Louisiana to New York, where he was elected to the New York State Assembly in 1841 and served two terms.

In 1844 Davezac campaigned in James Polk's campaign for president, making as many as sixty speeches on Polk's behalf and conducting a whistle-stop train tour from New York to five cities. In a speech in Baltimore, he gave a sample of the oratorical prowess for which he was known. When his Whig opponent derisively referred to him as a "foreigner" (no doubt because he spoke English with a pronounced French accent), Davezac made a withering reply:

> I am sorry to interrupt you, but I can permit no man to use such language in my presence. Judging from your appearance, I was an American citizen before you were born. I have a son, born an American citizen, older than you. As for myself, I have been four times naturalized. I was naturalized by the sanctity of the treaty of Louisiana, the highest form of law known to the Constitution. The rights of an American citizen were conferred upon me by the law creating the Territorial Government of Louisiana; and I was admitted to all the rights, blessings, and obligations which belong to you, my fellow citizens, by the law bringing the State of Louisiana into our glorious confederacy. . . . Sir, you look now as if you desired to know where and when was the fourth time of my naturalization, and who were my sponsors. The consecrated spot on which I received the rights of naturalization was the battle ground of New Orleans; the altar was victory, the baptismal water was blood and fire; Andrew Jackson was my god-father, and patriotism, freedom and glory my god-mothers.[24]

After Polk's election, Davezac was reappointed to his post of chargé d'affaires to the Netherlands, where he served from 1845 to 1850. He died in New York in 1851.

Final Assessments

Henry Stuart Foote, who knew Davezac socially, commented upon the man's appearance, intellect, and legal career in an unflattering way:

> I knew Mr. Davezac well, but only in social circles. There he did not shine conspicuously—being not a little coarse and obscene. His face, in which a geniality bordering on sensualism habitually sparkled, brought to my mind always the idea of a satyr, and there was in it an appearance of cunning and insincerity not a little disagreeable to behold. He had the credit of speaking with uncommon fluency, and of being quite effective in jury trials calling for ridicule and invective. I believe that he was never regarded as a deeply read lawyer or a man of more than ordinary literary culture.[25]

However, Jan Onofrio portrayed him with considerably more sympathy: "Of outstanding natural ability and charm, enjoying the esteem of Jackson, and for thirty years closely associated with Livingston, who was his constant mentor and during his early diplomatic career his anxious adviser, he was a striking and distinguished figure in contemporary Louisiana affairs. Yet his career presents somewhat of an enigma. Perhaps because of too volatile a nature, an inconstance of purpose, or lack of high ideals, he never attained the eminence which his intellectual endowments should have assured."[26]

Unfortunately, there is no mention of Davezac's translation of the Digest of 1808.

FIGURE 1. The Sala Capitular of the Cabildo. The small courtroom where H. P. Nugent's trial was held. John Elk III / Alamy.

FIGURE 2. Judge François-Xavier Martin of the Superior Court, presiding judge in the case of *Territory v. Nugent*. Courtesy of the Law Library of Louisiana, Louisiana Supreme Court.

FIGURE 3. Judge Joshua Lewis of the Superior Court, the target of Nugent's defamatory pamphlet. Courtesy of the Law Library of Louisiana, Louisiana Supreme Court.

FIGURE 4. Louis Moreau-Lislet, jurisconsult and codrafter of the Digest of Orleans (1808) and the Civil Code of 1825. Courtesy of the Grand Lodge of the State of Louisiana.

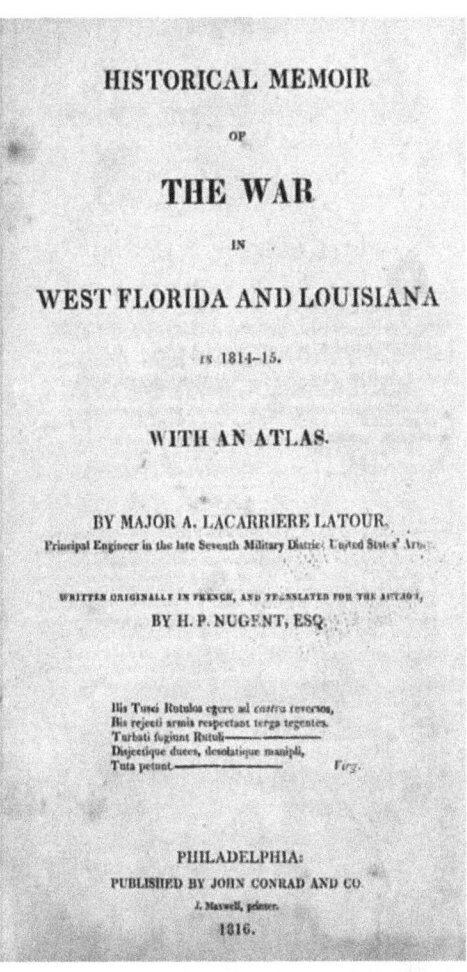

FIGURE 6. H. P. Nugent was the translator of Arsène LaCarrière Latour's *Historical Memoir of the War in West Florida and Louisiana 1814–1815*, which contains an account of the Battle of New Orleans. Archive.org.

FIGURE 5. James Brown (1766–1835) by Matthew Harris Jouett, photograph of oil on canvas portrait, ca. 1820, Liberty Hall Historic Site Collectons.

FIGURE 7. Julien Lalande Poydras, president of the Legislative Council and H. P. Nugent's close friend. Courtesy of the State Library of Louisiana.

FIGURE 8. Auguste Davezac de Castera, lawyer and translator of the Digest of Orleans. Courtesy of the New York Public Library.

FIGURE 9. Edward Livingston, legal mentor and brother-in-law of Auguste Davezac de Castera. Wikicommons.

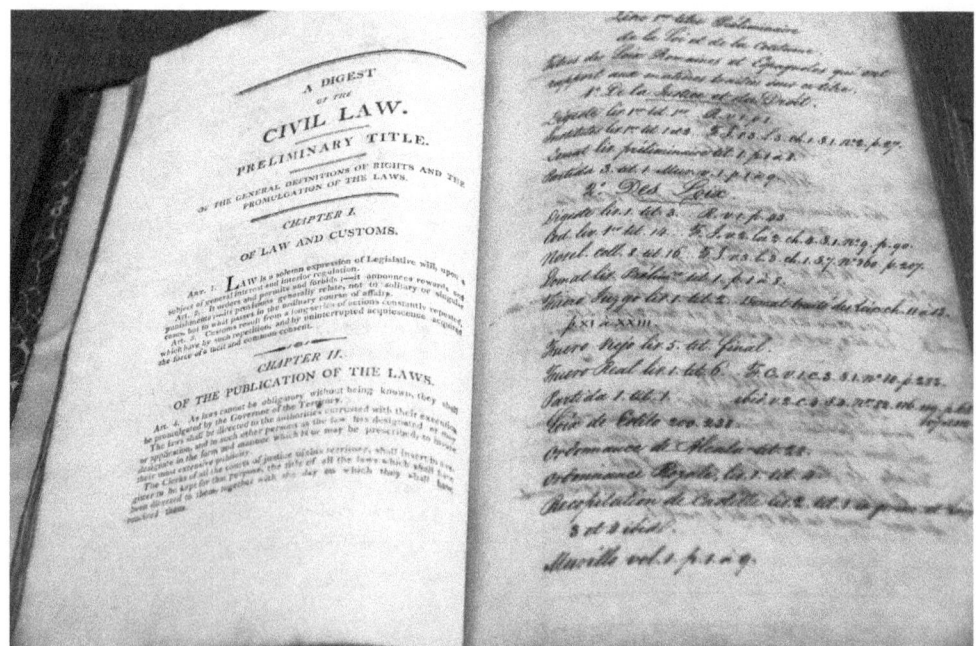

FIGURE 10. The Digest of Orleans of 1808, with Louis Moreau-Lislet's annotations. Courtesy of the Tulane Law Library.

FIGURE 11. Jean Domat, French scholar whose writings were one of the principal sources of the Digest of Orleans. Wikicommons.

FIGURE 12. Robert Joseph Pothier, French scholar whose treatise was translated into English by François-Xavier Martin. Alamy.

FIGURE 13. Sir William Blackstone's *Commentaries on the Laws of England* was a key reference book for the translators of the Digest of Orleans. By Thomas Gainsborough, ca. 1774. Courtesy of the Tate.

CHAPTER 5

Reexamining and Exhuming a Pioneer Translation

The names of the translators remained shrouded for over two centuries, but their translation was pronounced defective from the outset. No sooner had the ink dried than the translation was condemned as rife with errors by Governor W. C. C. Claiborne. The governor informed Secretary of State James Madison that the translation was "extremely incorrect" because the translators were unfamiliar with the English language: "This is attributable to the circumstance of the Work having been written in French, and the translation prepared by persons who were not well acquainted with the English Language." It is, however, doubtful that Governor Claiborne was personally competent to make these judgments. He did not speak French at that time, and though he was a lawyer, he had no training in civil law. Furthermore, he seemed unaware that one of the translators was a native speaker and actually quite familiar with the English language. His opinion was probably an echo of that of his advisors. Whatever the case, he proceeded to make a disturbing prediction—that the legislature would be forced to relinquish the goal of a bilingual code: "So erroneous does the translation appear to be that it will probably be necessary to declare by Law, that the French shall (solely) be considered the legal text."[1] That prophecy never materialized. The legislature never changed over to a French-only civil code, and it never called for a corrected translation to be made. Instead, it left the anglophone community at the mercy of the "extremely incorrect" English version for more than a hundred a fifty years, despite repeated calls for a revised translation. And in the course of time, many of the original errors were carried forward and perpetuated in the 1825 and 1870 civil codes. Legislative abstention inevitably left the problems of translation in the hands of the courts. It proved to be a lasting dilemma. On the one hand, the legislature originally decreed that the French and English texts had "equal authority," and there was to be no order of precedence: "That if, in any of the dispositions contained in the said digest, there should be found any obscurity or ambiguity, fault or omission, both the English and French texts shall be consulted, and shall mutually serve to the interpretation of one and the other."[2] On the other hand, as the disparities began to manifest themselves in actual cases, the courts found that it was necessary to establish an order of preference. Eventually, the judges adopted a "French-preference rule," which meant that in the event of conflict between the two texts, the French text would prevail.[3]

In a 1924 paper presented to the Louisiana Bar Association, Edward Dubuisson stated that the translations of the early codes, including that of 1808, were "very negligently executed, resulting in many gross faults of translation and perversions of the meaning of the legislator."[4] In his opinion, the translations were done so poorly that a general revision was still urgent and imperative. Dubuisson restricted himself to a few striking examples that he found ludicrous and amusing. His overall conclusion was that "even where the translations do not contain misleading errors, the vigor, the spirit, the clarity and finish of the originals are lost in the translations."[5] Roger Ward's assessment came to a similar conclusion: "Juxtaposition of the two different versions of the original Louisiana civil code reveals that the French edition is the superior of the two. Compiled and written by two men of extraordinary legal caliber, the French-language code is succinct, lucid, and internally consistent. The English version, on the other hand, is riddled with ambiguity, muddled, and inconsistent with its French counterpart."[6]

The accuracy of the translation was also carefully examined by Professor Joseph Dainow in the course of compiling his *1972 Compiled Edition of the Civil Codes of Louisiana*. Professor Dainow attempted to correct errors that he deemed to be "literal" mistakes, but he made no overall summary or classification of these mistakes, nor did he comment upon the quality of the translation in other respects. Like Dubuisson and Ward, Dainow apparently assumed that the translators' exclusive aim was to make a literal translation. His corrections always attempt to align the English version more closely to the literal meaning of the French text. His assumption in that regard, however, is to some extent unhistorical. In light of the *intentional* liberties, bold interpolations, and common-law equivalents that the present study uncovers, literalism could only have been one goal, not the exclusive one.

There is no reason to take the reader through the hundreds of errors that Dainow found. His meticulous work has been invaluable to the profession and to the present study, but I believe there are more interesting things to be learned when we approach the translation in a more general way. It will be shown, for example, that there is a telltale taxonomy to the errors, that is, a pattern of irregularity that makes the linguistic signatures of each translator discernible. The pattern discloses the boundaries of their individual contributions and tells an unusual tale of two translations masquerading as one—two incoherent and inconsistent parts that have been stitched together to make a whole. The reexamination also discloses the existence of a third translator, a previously unknown British source from which nearly sixty provisions were copied verbatim. More importantly, the reexamination will show the degree to which the translation catered to the common-law culture of the early judges and immigrant lawyers. Here we shall find that the translators freely substituted what they believed were equivalent common-law terms and terminology, with the result that from the start they presented a version of civil law already partly mingled with common law.

Setting the Scene: A Neglected Translation at the Margin of a Rich Literature

In setting the scene for the reexamination in this chapter, it may be of interest to ask what a study of the translation brings to various scholarly debates about the digest of 1808. The digest has a rich and voluminous literature; it is far larger than the literature surrounding the later civil codes of 1825 or 1870. Very little of this outpouring, however, has concerned the translation. It has been kept in the wings, at the margins of scholarly interest.

This is not the place to pass this literature in full review, for only parts of it intersect with insights from the translation.[7] Most of the scholarship relates to the drafting of the jurisconsults Moreau-Lislet and Brown and ignores the impact of the translation. For example, in the debate between Professor Robert Pascal of Louisiana State University and Professor Rodolfo Batiza of Tulane University over the origins and sources of the digest, the translation was not discussed and played no role in either substantiating, refuting, or countering the central claims. Both sides conceded that Louis Casimir Moreau-Lislet and James Brown made extensive verbatim and almost verbatim recourse to two French models, the Code Napoléon (1804) and the Projet du Gouvernement (1800), in confecting the digest, but they deeply disagreed as to what that proved about the "true sources" of those provisions.

The basic reason why there has been so much dispute about the sources of the digest is that neither Moreau-Lislet nor Brown kept a journal. They wrote no *exposé des motifs* explaining what they were thinking during the drafting, where they obtained their source material, why they made certain choices (e.g., why Blackstone? why Jean Domat?), or whether they intended to make the code substantively Spanish (as Professor Pascal believed) or substantively French (as Professor Batiza famously argued). The truth is, we are in the dark because there are no contemporaneous notes of their intentions. Perhaps the only insight we have into the opaque mind of Moreau-Lislet lies in his hand-annotated copy of the digest, which he composed in 1814, which is now frequently referred to as the "de la Vergne volume" after the family that held it in trust over the years, and which some scholars have attempted to read (disingenuously, I believe) *as if* it were in fact an *exposé des motifs*.[8]

Both drafters were public figures in their day and held nearly every office of trust in Louisiana. To my knowledge, however, they made no private or public comment during their lifetimes on the subject of their sources or their intentions. Interestingly, however, many distinguished contemporaries, some of whom were quite close to the drafting process, did comment about the actual sources. Edward Livingston, François-Xavier Martin, Henry Bullard, Jeremiah Brown, and John Hughes all publicly stated that the jurisconsults had codified the French system, not the Spanish.[9] Indeed, John Hughes, a member of the legislature who served on the code oversight committee, declared from the floor of the House: "That code is not the ancient law of the territory, of which it purports to be a digest, but almost verbatim *the new system of France—the Napoleon Code*" (his italics). The newspaper that reported Hughes's speech repeated his claim: "It is a lamentable fact that the civil law now in force in this territory is not a digest of the ancient laws of Louisiana, but of the present imperial law of France."[10] Furthermore, another New Orleans newspaper, *La Lanterne magique*, republished an article that circulated in Paris in which the author called the digest a "paraphrase" of the Code Napoléon and praised Moreau-Lislet's "glorious plagiary":

> The Province of Louisiana, though separated for the present, from the GREAT EMPIRE, by a certain concurrence of events, continues to evince the highest veneration for all our political institutions. *To avoid the barbarous yoke of a Gothick system* of jurisprudence called the common law of England, the principles of the civil law have been expressly and exclusively adopted as the basis of a new code which is shortly to be promulgated in that Province. *M. Louis Moreau Lislet, a French jurisconsult, has the honor of digesting this code; which in fact is a paraphrase of the Napoleon code.* . . . We presume that Mr. Moreau thought it necessary to disguise *the glorious plagiary*, lest he might excite the national jealousies of his new fellow citizens. And he has disguised it effectually. (emphasis added)[11]

If the public statements of leading lawyers, judges, and legislators were untrue characterizations of the digest's sources, or demeaned the reputation of the codifiers, one might have thought that Moreau-Lislet and Brown would have refuted the claims or at least responded to them. Significantly, there was no public response.

Rodolfo Batiza's research proved that the digest was indeed the first reception of the French civil code outside of France. He amply corroborated the claim of "glorious plagiary" by showing that more than fourteen hundred articles of the digest were directly copied, either verbatim or almost verbatim, from the *code civil des français* (or Code Napoléon) of 1804 and its *avant-projet* (or Projet du Gouvernement) of 1800. He further demonstrated that the jurisconsults borrowed extensively from the classic writings of French authors Jean Domat and Robert Pothier, so that in the aggregate about 85 percent of the digest was taken from French legislation and treatises. His research also identified a certain number of Spanish sources, though a smaller number, and revealed that the redactors had even drawn from Sir William Blackstone's *Commentaries on the Laws of England*. Professor Batiza gave exact numbers for these sources: Projet du Gouvernement, 807 provisions; French civil code of 1804, 709 provisions; Domat, 175 provisions; Pothier, 113 provisions; *Febrero Adicionado* (a work by the Spanish writer Febrero), 52 provisions; Blackstone, 25 provisions; Louisiana Act of April 6, 1806, on marriage, 16 provisions; Custom of Paris (a French enactment codifying the customary law that developed in the region of Paris), 9 provisions.[12]

The recent research by Seth Brostoff suggests that the indebtedness to French law is greater than Batiza believed or conceded. Brostoff has identified nearly one hundred additional provisions copied verbatim or almost verbatim from French legal encyclopedias, all of which were omitted from Batiza's analysis. Indeed, some of these French encyclopedia–based provisions were wrongly identified by Batiza as Spanish sources, and thus Brostoff's research tends to reduce the proportional importance of Spanish law.[13]

Robert Pascal dismissed Batiza's research as purely "philological," arguing that it dwelt upon word and phrase analysis and did not trace the substantive law itself. "If this substance is predominantly Spanish-Roman," he wrote, "then it does not matter that it is expressed in terms French and English rather than Spanish and Latin, or that the specific terms employed often were inspired by, adapted from, or even copied from texts on French or other systems of law."[14] Insisting on this *substance-over-form* distinction and emphasizing the drafters' instructions to maintain the law of Spain "in force," he concluded that the digest was in reality "a Spanish girl in a French dress."[15]

It is fair to say, however, that if the English translation had been investigated and factored into this famous debate (it was not), inevitably the "dress" would have looked less French and the "girl" would have looked less Spanish. The common-law cast of the translation operates as a counterpoint to both sides' contentions.

Understandably, Professor Batiza made no attempt to trace the sources of the English translation, perhaps because it could seem odd to think that a translation might have any source other than the French texts under translation. It turns out, however, that the Nugent/Davezac translation had a number of extrinsic sources, for example, an old English translation of Domat dated 1722, old statutes, law dictionaries and treatises, and particularly Blackstone's *Commentaries on the Laws of England*. The present investigation concludes that Blackstone's presence in the code proves to be greater than previously thought or acknowledged. His shadow now appears not only in the places originally identified but in common-law words of art (technical or specialized language understood by professionals but not laymen) repeatedly used (e.g., "obligor," "profits," "inheritance"), which Nugent and Davezac introduced *interstitially* as conceptual equivalents of civil law terms.[16]

These references to Blackstone undermine to some extent the ingenious theory that verbatim borrowings are merely philological and furnish only a convenient form of words to express Spanish substantive law. To be sure, Professor Pascal applied his substantive-law argument solely to the French texts of the digest in response to the findings of Batiza, but presumably he would have found it more difficult to apply that argument to the borrowings of an anglicized translation. Unlike Moreau-Lislet and Brown, the translators did not receive instructions of any kind from the legislature and had no mandate to maintain the law of Spain "in force." Their purpose in introducing common-law terms and legal ideas would not have been to fulfill instructions directed to Moreau-Lislet and Brown, nor to clothe Spanish substance in English dress, but simply to communicate in the language best understood by the anglophone bench and bar.

Finally, the nature of the translation can be assessed from the perspective of the so-called clash of legal traditions theory, the basic theme of a classic work by George Dargo.[17] An anglicized translation may be seen as the product of opposed social forces. It is a mirror of the old cultural, legal, and linguistic fault lines of early Louisiana society. Certainly, it was shaped to some extent by the effects of those divisions. At the same time, it served as a means to accommodate, reconcile, or bridge legal differences and to overcome communication gaps between the traditions. The art of translation became a subtle means of blending laws and language and of reducing the old divisions. Mixed jurisdictions like Louisiana, Scotland, and South Africa are known for hybrid laws, sui generis norms, and original creations.[18] The 1808 translation is another example of these uncatalogued creations.

Literal Translation versus Legal Transposition

The digest translation cannot be considered a simple literal translation of civil law from French into English. Most of it, to be sure, consists of literal translation, yet in many telltale instances it is something more complex and difficult to describe. Often enough it appears to be a project to translate civil law concepts into common-law equivalents for the benefit of an anglophone legal audience. Ordinary English—the everyday language of nonlawyers—might have been considered a sufficiently neutral medium to express civil law rules and concepts. A strictly literal translation that sent an untutored anglophone reader back to civilian sources like Domat, Pothier, and Febrero for needed definitions and elucidation might have been attempted and perhaps was actually expected by the French legal community of 1808. A literal translation, however, would have put the burden upon the anglophone reader to revert to civilian roots and sources in Spanish, French, and Latin to understand or clarify the rules and principles of the digest. A literal translation in ordinary English would have kept almost all interpretive autonomy with the French text. It would have given preference and priority to the French texts; therefore, it would have favored the dominance of the French-language community and its legal culture.

It takes the reader only a few pages to realize, however, that in many cases the translators abandoned neutral, straightforward English. They readily inserted terms and phrases drawn from the Anglo-American legal culture that had no equivalence in the French language or in the general vocabulary of the civil law. Thus we find that certain French words have been replaced by common-law terms scattered in the provisions, as in the following instances:

> *attorney in fact* (translating "procureur" and/or "mandataire") (arts. 7, 10, 13, p. 422)[19]
> *chattels* (translating "des biens") (art. 9, p. 342)
> *consideration* (translating "le prix") (art. 60, p. 466)[20]
> *joint and several obligation* (translating "obligation solidaire") (art. 97, p. 273; art. 32, p. 426)
> *loan on bottomry* (translating "le prêt á grosse aventure") (art. 1, p. 420)

54   CHAPTER FIVE

> *parol evidence* (translating "preuve par temoin")
>   (art. 241, p. 310; art. 242, p. 311)
> *sales by cant* (translating "licitation") (chap. 6, pp. 366–67)[21]
> *separation from bed and board* (translating "la séparation de corps")
>   (art. 1, p. 30)
> *the landlord* (translating "le propriétaire") (art. 74, p. 468)

These words are not, I would submit, ordinary expressions of the English language but rather ordinary terms of the Anglo-American common law.[22] Their presence in the translation well illustrates the truism that legal English terminology is a specific language within a language used by legal professionals and that a good command of ordinary English does not necessarily make one proficient in legal English.

It is useful to pause here and ask why the translators deemed it appropriate to engraft English law terminology onto the civil law. This requires a short digression, first about contemporary translation practices and second about the nature and needs of the Louisiana bench and bar.

Contemporary Precedent: The Example of the Early Statutes

The transposition of French into common-law equivalents was not unprecedented in the territory. In the early statutes, it was apparently established practice to juxtapose common-law terms in translating from the French. The bilingual acts of the legislature for 1804–8 were conspicuous in their use of common-law concepts that had no *literal* connection to the underlying French version of the statute. Translators attached to the legislature had used, for example, the following words:

> *chattels* (translating "marchandises")[23]
> *indenture* (translating "engagé")[24]
> *tenement* (translating "propriété")[25]
> *lien* (translating "hypothèque")[26]
> *valuable consideration* (translating "un prix convenable")[27]
> *attorney in fact* (translating "fondé de pouvoir par document authentique")[28]

In light of this practice, the Nugent/Davezac translation could be said to follow the lead of the legislature itself. If contemporary practice was an important influence, however, it might suggest that the process of mixing the two laws was, from the beginning, almost instinctively and unreflectively carried out. In the next section, however, I will attempt to show that there was in fact a conscious design to this process.

The Pedagogic Undercurrent

The pedagogic nature of the Louisiana civil code of 1825 was once described by Mitchell Franklin in a brilliant summation in which he contrasted the far lengthier, example-filled pages of that code with the concise and commanding positivism of its shorter model, the French civil code.[29] The 1825 civil code contained 3,522 articles, in contrast to the French civil code of 1804, with merely 2,281 articles. "The difference in the length of the two codes," Franklin wrote, "was a difference, in no small way, between a code that was a code, and a code that was a code, a law-school and doctrine all at once."[30] Franklin did not make a similar assertion about the Digest of 1808, for the latter was indeed shorter than the French civil code, and it contained far less of what he regarded as pedagogic material.[31] Like other scholars of the codes, Franklin was primarily focused on the texts drafted by the codifiers and tended to ignore what was contained in the translation. Once our attention shifts to the translation, however, it is immediately evident that the translation has an independent educational or pedagogic purpose. By this I mean to say that the digest presents a kind of didactic bilingualism in which the translation (without verbal prompts from the French text) is the medium by which a certain number of common-law ideas and terminology were embedded for the convenience and/or enlightenment of anglophone readers.

Wendell Holmes and Symeon Symeonides saw this purpose at work when they examined the provisions on mandate.[32] They noticed that in English translation the French word *mandat* simply disappeared from view. The word was not translated, even though at a literal level the English word "mandate" was perhaps an exact fit. Instead of using mandate, the translators opted to retain the French word *procuration*, and in an effort to elucidate that word's meaning in English, they subjoined the common-law expression "letter of attorney."[33] The authors commented on the significance of this addition: "The addition of the term 'letter of attorney' was an understandable attempt to explain to a primarily English-speaking readership the meaning of the rather obscure French word *procuration*. More interesting was the fact that the English text did not contain the word 'mandate.' This, however, was not a mistranslation."[34] Their conclusion is accurate, and further examples can be given. This was no mistranslation. It was the deliberate substitution of a common-law expression.

The same approach is repeatedly followed in the topical headings placed above the provisions in English. For example, the headings to a provision on solidary obligations show bold differences in their French and English versions:

French: "Des Obligations Solidaires"
English: "Of Obligations *In Solido* or Jointly and Severally"
   (sec. 4, p. 278)

In the above example, Nugent and Davezac lengthened the heading in order to inform the anglophone reader that solidary obligations have the same functional meaning as "joint and several" obligations at common law. The shorter French heading was of course not the source of this additional information. So the francophone reader did not receive the same information as the anglophone reader.[35] The translators saw no problem in giving one legal audience more information, or at least different information, than the other.

Other headings were conceptually anglicized in a similar way:

French: "De la Nature et de la Forme du Mandat"
English: "Of the Nature of Proxies, Mandates and Commissions"[36]

Note how the words "proxies" and "commissions" spring from thin air. They serve as synonyms or analogues to convey the concept of mandate to an English-speaking reader. As noted previously, "mandate" is arguably a good word in both languages. Yet the judgment of the translators was that "mandate" alone might mislead or perhaps fail to resonate with an English speaker.[37] The work of synonyms is to transpose the concept into a common-law register.

The same objective was pursued in another heading on mandate. Here the translators used thirteen words to express what the French heading stated in four words, and the expression "attorney in fact" served as a synonym for a mandatary:

> French: "Des Obligations du Mandant"[38]
> English: "Of the Obligations of the Principal Who Acts by His Attorney in Fact"

A strategy of common-law equivalency was at work when the translators added the archaic phrase "sales by cant" to a heading on licitation:

> French: "De la Licitation"
> English: "Of Sales by Cant or Auction"[39]

To understand the rationale for a "conceptually anglicized translation," we must consider the background and training of the intended audience. Nugent and Davezac were conscious of the native language and legal culture of a majority of the bench and bar of the early nineteenth century. The anglophone bench and bar, it is believed, were the primary audiences they were attempting to reach.

The Culture and Needs of the Anglophone Lawyers

The Nugent/Davezac translation was devised primarily for American-trained lawyers who could better understand unfamiliar civilian concepts through the substitution of correlative terms and synonyms.[40] This approach, whatever one may think of its merits or demerits, makes the translation an interesting mixed-jurisdiction artifact.

Given the makeup and culture of Louisiana's first bench and bar, an anglicized translation was neither an unreasonable nor illogical undertaking. We should remember that the Louisiana bar came into existence only five years before the digest was enacted. There was no practicing bar before 1803. Under Spanish rule (1769–1803), *Luisiana* was a vast province without *abogados* (lawyers). The few legal professionals who lived in New Orleans, the capital city, held quasi-governmental positions, such as the *letrados* (doctors of law) who served as assessors assisting the *alcaldes ordinarios* (ordinary judges) and the *procuradores del numero* (prosecutors) appointed by the courts.[41] In Elizabeth Gaspard's words, "During the colonial period, the few lawyers who lived in Louisiana were officials of the metropole sent by the crown to assist the colonial administrators."[42] Hans

Baade confirms there was never more than one *letrado* in the capital at a given time and usually no more than two or three *procuradores* or *escribanos* (notaries). Apart from these functionaries, no organized legal profession existed prior to 1803.[43]

Soon after the purchase, conditions changed dramatically. A stream of legal practitioners from the United States and abroad flooded the territory. In a study of this legal migration for the years 1803–12, Kenneth Aslakson counted up to sixty-four lawyers in New Orleans alone.[44] About two-thirds arrived in a rush between 1803 and 1805. The majority (about 56 percent) were anglophone Americans (meaning their first language was English, even if they spoke or understood other languages).[45] Moreover, after 1812 the Americans steadily increased their numerical advantage.[46] The francophone members of the bar (meaning their first language was French) were less numerous and comprised about 37 percent.[47] Only four of them were native-born Louisianians.

Almost without exception, these early lawyers and judges had no previous experience with codes, codal interpretation, or civilian learning. Typically, they had "read" law as apprentices in chambers and were not university trained. They were unacquainted with the sources, the writings, and the vocabulary that framed the codal provisions of the digest. George Dargo wrote "the average American attorney coming to Louisiana with two or three volumes of English law was bewildered by what he encountered."[48] It was not unexpected that their first encounter with codified civil law would be confusing, and it was not unreasonable for the legislature to attempt to minimize the confusion.

All of the first judges and justices of the territory and state had common-law training and labored under a similar civil law deficit.[49] For example, François-Xavier Martin of North Carolina (but born in Marseilles) was a printer and translator who had also served in the North Carolina legislature. He had "read" for the North Carolina bar by mastering common-law materials. His judicial experience before an appointment to the Superior Court of the Territory of Orleans was in the adjoining Mississippi Territory. He was appointed to the Louisiana Supreme Court in 1815 and served on that court for the next thirty-one years, the last ten as chief justice. George Mathews of Georgia learned law in the law offices of his brother in Augusta, Georgia. He was a judge in the Mississippi Territory for two years before his appointment in 1806 to the Superior

Court of the Territory of Orleans. He sat on the Louisiana Supreme Court from 1813 to 1836. Joshua Lewis also had a common-law background. He was born in Virginia, graduated from Washington and Lee, and practiced law for a time in Lexington, Kentucky. He was appointed to the Superior Court in 1806, and after statehood he became judge of the First Judicial District in New Orleans, where he remained till his death in 1833. Alexander Porter, an Irish immigrant who settled in Tennessee, practiced law in that state before coming to Louisiana. He sat on the Louisiana Supreme Court from 1820 to 1833.

The Nugent/Davezac translation of 1808 made concessions and accommodations for the training and culture of the bench and bar and possibly the American merchants as well. The translators did not hesitate to anglicize the translation when they thought it was appropriate to the "communicative situation."[50] In general, the anglophone bar was limited in languages and lacked familiarity with the civil law tradition. This seems to explain not only the interjection of common-law terminology in the translation but why the first codes came equipped with a number of reader-friendly aids not usually found on the Continent, such as definitional articles placed at the beginning of titles, alphabetically arranged indexes in French and English, and a self-contained thesaurus of code concepts succinctly defined.[51]

Of this pioneer period, it has been said that "opportunities for lawyers seemed endless, regardless of a prospective attorney's background or preparation. There were few rules to control admission to the bar, and the question of what constituted adequate training was left open. Ambitious men were unfettered in their efforts to use the law as a springboard into other areas of Louisiana society."[52] Liberal rules on admission facilitated the rapid expansion of the bar.[53] When the first wave of lawyers arrived between 1803 and 1807, the qualifications for practice were quite minimal. An applicant needed only to be a U.S. citizen, twenty-one years of age, and a resident in the territory for one year.[54] A later statute stipulated that lawyers should have good moral character and no prior convictions, and they should refrain from fomenting suits or accepting land or property as a fee.[55] A Superior Court rule later split the legal profession into two groups, attorneys and counsels, with different functions allocated to each branch. Every lawyer was required to elect whether he would be a counsellor or an attorney.[56] The bifurcation, however, was short-lived, and by the time of statehood the profession was unified once again. The Louisiana Supreme Court rules after statehood continued a liberal policy. Extending comity nationwide, it would examine any candidate who already held a license to practice in another state or territory, and it would examine first-time applicants who had been supervised by a practicing attorney for at least three years.[57]

George Dargo found evidence of widespread hostility toward lawyers in Louisiana in this period.[58] In 1804 Pierre Derbigny, who was successively a judge, a codifier, and finally governor, lamented the "prodigious number of lawyers" and the steep increase in litigation. He was disturbed by the actions of greedy attorneys "digging among the ashes of faded causes."[59] The translator Henry Paul Nugent, writing anonymously in 1809, declared that chicanery and fraud among local lawyers were rampant and notorious. Citizens, he wrote, were being "cruelly harassed by barretors [litigation stirrers] and champertors [sharers of litigation proceeds]," and "lawyers are getting all the landed property in their hands; and it is the common belief and I think well founded, that they encourage frauds of all kinds, making knavery to set law at defiance, provided the lawyers share the gains." He placed Edward Livingston at "the head of the brigands."[60]

Conclusion on the Bijural Translation

However the idea for a bijural translation actually originated, it was surely a consequential step in the birth of civil law in Louisiana, for the act of translation (as opposed to its original redaction in French) produced an immediate and almost unnoticed reception of common-law ideas. This meant that the civil law arrived on the scene preemptively mixed and already resonating with common-law terms and ideas. This unheralded reception was linguistically one-sided. The common law was expressed exclusively in one language (English) and was not found in the other (French). Arguably, one could say this was not "translation" so much as an unacknowledged means of legislation. It is also interesting to note that the selection of equivalent English legal terms was carried out by legally untrained translators rather than by the redactors Moreau-Lislet and Brown. The delicate task of transposing from one tradition to another, it is believed, would normally call for a sophisticated understanding of comparative law. Unless Nugent and Davezac consulted with experienced advisors, the task would appear to have been well beyond their preparation or qualifications. Based on their biographies, neither man had a thorough knowledge of the territory's civil law, let alone knowledge of the two major legal traditions that it straddled. Neither was admitted to the bar in 1807, and neither was fully trained either in civil law or common law. Davezac, whose first training was in medicine, had not completed his legal apprenticeship and was not eligible for admission to the bar in 1807–8. He was not a native speaker in the target language, and his later specialization in criminal law, where apparently he excelled, was not particularly relevant to the civil law he was called upon to translate. For his part, Nugent was a native speaker, a newspaper editor, a former dancer, a language teacher, and a translator, but his knowledge of civil law and common law may not have been greater than that of a well-educated person.

A Notable Invention:
The Distinction between Obligors and Obligees

The jurisconsults of the digest used the classic words "créancier et débiteur" (creditor and debtor) in articulating the rules and principles of the law of obligations. That terminology has a venerable pedigree in classical civil law and continues to be used in the French civil code.[61]

In a bold departure, the translators introduced the words "obligor" and "obligee" in place of "debtor" and "creditor" (arts. 42–45, p. 268). At the time of the experiment, obligor and obligee were obscure and musty English law terms that were rarely used even in common-law books. The usage that existed was confined to the discrete subject of English bonds.[62] The terms had almost no currency in classic common-law works, such as those by Lord Coke and Thomas Wood, or even in old dictionaries, for, as just mentioned, they were deployed solely in connection with the subject of bonds.[63] The most likely source or inspiration for the translators may have been Blackstone's *Commentaries on the Laws of England*, for we know that it was highly prized in early Louisiana, and both translators made frequent use of it.[64] In Blackstone's treatment of an "an *obligation* or bond" (his italics), he employed the obligor/obligee terminology repeatedly and with emphasis.[65] The translators repurposed obligor and obligee into a set of paired opposites at the service of the civil law. The French language, even today, has no comparable vocabulary.[66]

An apparent virtue of the obligor/obligee distinction and perhaps a feature that attracted the translators is that it is perfectly abstract and applicable across many contexts in the field of obligations. Accordingly, we might have expected the translators to deploy the experiment widely, perhaps in dozens of situations where the creditor/debtor terminology was used in the French texts.[67] But for some unclear reason they restricted the use of the neologism to just five articles. We are left to speculate about the reason for this reluctance. Obviously, it was not because the words *créancier* and *débiteur* were in any way difficult to render into English. Nor does it seem that the substance or subject matter of the five articles in question was singular or difficult and demanded on that account the invention of a neologism.

The likely reason for the translators' restraint is that they were quite unsure of themselves, having never encountered or used these terms before. This is borne out by a singular fact. In every instance where they applied the new terminology, they applied it precisely backward and mistakenly, thus producing legal nonsense. In each instance, the French version suddenly waged war with the English translation. Obviously, had they made any wider application, they simply would have extended their errors. In light of the examples set forth below, one has to conclude that the translator(s) were experimenting with words they did not understand.

ART. 42, P. 268

Every obligation to do or not to do, resolves itself into damages, in case of non execution on the part of the *obligee* [sic].

Toute obligation, de faire ou de ne pas faire, se résout en dommages intérêts, en cas d'inexécution de la part du *débiteur*.

ART. 43, P. 269

Nevertheless the *obligor* [sic] has a right to require that whatever has been done in contravention to the agreement, be done; and he may be authorised to undo it at the expence of the *obligee* [sic] without forfeiting his right to damages, if the case gives him a claim to them.

Néanmoins, le *créancier* a le droit de demander, que ce qui aurait été fait, par contravention à l'engagement, soit détruit; et il peut se faire autoriser à le détruire, aux dépens du *débiteur*, sans préjudice des dommages et intérêts, s'il y a lieu.

ART. 44, P. 268

The *obligor* [sic] may also, in case of non execution, be authorized to cause the obligation to be executed by himself at the expence of the *obligee* [sic].

Le *créancier* peut aussi, en cas d'inexécution, être autorisé à faire exécuter lui-meme l'obligation, aux dépens du *débiteur*.

ART. 116, P. 282

If the affair for which the debt has been contracted in solido, concerns only one of the *co-obligees* [sic] in solido,[68] that one is liable for the whole debt towards the other co-debtors, who with regard to him, are considered only as his securities.

Si l'affaire, pour laquelle la dette a été contractée solidairement, ne conernait que l'un des *co-obligés* solidaires, celui-ci serait tenu de toute la dette, vis-à-vis des autres codebiteurs, qui ne seraient considérés, par rapport á lui, que comme ses cautions.

ART. 136, P. 286

An obligation may be discharged by any person concerned in it, such as a *co-obligee* [sic] or a security.

ART. 136, P. 287

Une obligation peut être acquittée par toute personne qui y est intéressée, telle qu'un *co-obligé*, ou une caution.

One might have supposed that blunders of this magnitude would have destroyed the experiment in utero. As mentioned earlier, it was the maiden occasion on which these English words ventured out of the context denominated "bonds." Given the embarrassing results, the lesson learned might have been to return them and leave them there. Writing decades later, the legal philosopher John Austin, probably unaware of developments in Louisiana, expressed doubt that the words "obligor" and "obligee" could ever be uprooted from their historic context and deployed as general substantives.[69] But that was not to be the Louisiana experience nor the eventual lesson for English-speaking civilians generally. Within a few years Louis Moreau-Lislet and Henry Carleton, in their translation of *Las siete partidas*, made use of the obligor and obligee terminology in several instances (*partida* 7, *título* 43, *ley* 2, p. 1226), and the translators of the 1825 Louisiana civil code increased the application to twenty-three provisions.[70] That code even provided a formal definition of obligor and obligee in its final article.[71] Thus despite a stumbling start in 1808, the new terminology finally took hold to the point that it has flourished in modern times. It is now a commonplace among English-speaking civilians around the world.[72] Thus, it seems that one of the civil law's most useful expressions owes its existence to a seminal experiment by the translators of 1808.

Insights from Telltale Mistakes: The Mistranslation of *Fruits* and "Profits"

A systematic word choice by one of the translators (not both) left a string of clues concerning his identity, his modus operandi, and the parts of the digest he translated on his own. This translator consistently equated the French word *fruits* (which bears a technical meaning in the law of property) with the English word "profits." In so doing, he unwittingly dismantled the traditional division between natural fruits, industrial fruits, and civil fruits. His translation created the anomalous triptych—natural profits, industrial profits, and civil profits—and as we shall soon see, the error spawned a considerable number of hilarious provisions that will not bear reading aloud. Remarkably, this "error" (if indeed it was not intentional) became so deeply etched in the law that it passed unnoticed into the 1825 and 1870 civil codes and provoked litigation well into the twentieth century.[73]

> ART. 8, P. 112
>
> The usufructuary has a right to enjoy *all sorts of profits*, whether natural or the produce of industry or civil, proceeding from the object whose use belongs to him.
>
> ART. 8, P. 113
>
> L'usufruitier a le droit de jouir de *toutes les espèces de fruits* soit naturels, soit industriels, soit civils, que peut produire l'objet dont il a l'usufruit.
>
> ART. 9, P. 112
>
> *Natural profits* are such as are the spontaneous produce of the earth, the increase of cattle are likewise natural profits.[74] The profits which result from industry bestowed on a piece of ground, are those which are obtained by cultivation.

ART. 9, P. 113

Les fruits naturels sont ceux qui sont le produit spontané de la terre. Le produit et le croit des animaux sont aussi des fruits naturels. Les fruits industriels d'un fonds sont ceux qu'on en obtient par la culture.

ART. 10, P. 112

Civil profits are the rents of house, the interests on money which is due, the arrears of rents or annuities [sic].[75]

ART. 10, P. 113

Les fruits civils sont les loyers de maison, les intérêts des sommes exigibles, les arréarages des rentes.[76]

The conflation of fruits and profits had the unintended consequence of sometimes enlarging the rights of a usufructuary and sometimes increasing the husband's control over community property, as shown in the texts below.

ART. 64, P. 336

This partnership or community consists of the *profits* of all the effects of which the husband has the administration and enjoyment.

ART. 64, P. 337

Cette société, ou communauté, se compose des *fruits* de tous les biens dont le mari a l'administration et la jouissance.

The translator may have been unaware that the meaning of fruits extended only to those kinds of products (crops, rents, offspring of animals, etc.) that arise periodically and cause no alteration of the principal thing's substance, whereas profits simply suggests some sort of patrimonial increase and may be derived from all manners of operations, including those that deplete the thing or alter its substance, for example, the cutting down of trees or the mining of ore.[77]

Yet under another hypothesis, it may be wrong on our part to call this an error of translation. Perhaps this was a case in which a common-law word of art ("profits"), as understood within its own technical limits under the law of "waste," was inserted for the benefit of common-law jurists. When restricted by the concept of waste, profits may come very close to the technical meaning of fruits at civil law. In an important essay, Sally Richardson has pointed out that in comparing the rights of usufructuaries to life tenants, "fruits, as understood in the civil law, are the equivalent of profits in the common law."[78] Indeed, Blackstone, an author to whom Nugent and Davezac frequently turned, made the two terms sound equivalent by stating: "For he [the life tenant] hath a right to the full enjoyment and use of the land, *and all it's* [sic] *profits, during his estate therein. But he is not permitted to cut down timber or do other waste upon the premises*; for the destruction of such things, as are *not the temporary profits* of the tenement, is not necessary for the tenant's complete enjoyment of his estate."[79] Rather than call this a mistake, it is entirely possible, then, that the translator in question was satisfied that the two terms were equivalent and saw an advantage rather than an impropriety in inserting the common-law expression into the civil law text.

It is revealing, however, that the second translator (not being sure who is who, I will simply refer to him as the second translator) did not conflate fruits with profits and made no attempt to insert a common-law word of art. The sharp difference in their approach is a first step in discerning the existence of two linguistic signatures in the translation. The second translator simply decided to use the English word "fruit" as the proper translation of the French word *fruits*. His superior approach leads to an insight into the working methods of the translators. Apparently, the two men divided the task into respective parts. The mistakes or interpolations of the first translator were not compared for consistency or accuracy with the parts correctly translated by the second. Neither man revised or crosschecked the work of the other. From this and other evidence to be advanced in the following sections, we uncover a bifurcated translation in which the vast majority of the errors—whether stylistic, syntactical, or conceptual—were clustered in certain sections but not in others.

In the section below, there is more evidence of the same bifurcation. Here, the translators divided over the meaning of the French term *héritage*, but once again an apparent error on the part of one could be in reality the insertion of a common-law term into the translation.

Misunderstanding *Héritage* to Mean "Inheritance"

To someone perhaps unaware of French property law (or heedless of the shifting meaning of words in different subject areas), the French word *héritage* might be translated by its first dictionary meaning, "inheritance" (i.e., property that passes by succession). Unfortunately, one of the two translators repeatedly gave this meaning to the term in his translation of property law articles. His translation was illogical and inappropriate because he was translating property law articles having nothing to do with the subject of successions. He was translating texts that consistently called for *héritage* to be understood in its second dictionary meaning, in which it connotes a corporeal immovable, whether inherited or not. That is the consistent meaning attributed to *héritage* in the property articles of the French civil code and in the doctrinal sources from which those articles were taken (art. 20, p. 114). Thus, the appropriate English equivalent for *héritage* might be the word "estate" or, better still, immovable property. This misconception created a host of meaningless code provisions, and these errors were passed down to the later codes of 1825 (article 547) and 1870 (article 544) and remained law in the twentieth century. Some of the anomalous results can be seen in the examples below:

ART. 18, P. 114

Accordingly he may cut trees on land of which he has the usufruct ... provided he act in those respects as a prudent father, and so as that *the inheritance* be not thereby rendered entirely barren or useless.

Ainsi il peut faire des coupes de bois sur le fonds dont il a l'usufruit ... pourvu que ce soit en bon père de famille et de manière que *l'héritage* ne soit pas par là rendu totalement sterile ou inutile.

ART. 20, P. 114

The usufructuary enjoys the right of services, ways, or others due to *the inheritance* of which he has the usufruct, and if *this inheritance* is enclosed within the other lands ... the way must be gratuitously furnished to the usufructuary by the proprietor of the said lands or by his heirs.

L'usufruitier jouit des droits de servitude, de passage ou autres dus a *l'héritage* dont il a l'usufruit, et si *cet héritage* se trouve enclavé dans les autres possessions ... le passage doit être fourni gratuitement à l'usufruitier par le propriétaire ou par ses héritiers.

These articles obviously make no sense in ordinary English. They force upon the reader bizarre ideas like an *enclosed* inheritance and a *barren and useless* inheritance. Yet there is another possible way to interpret these provisions so that they make perfect sense, but only when directed to the presuppositions of a common-law lawyer. This interpretation requires us to remember once again that the Nugent/Davezac translation caters to an anglophone audience with a common-law background, and here the translator has apparently adopted Blackstone's sense of "inheritance" as his guide. In Blackstone's treatment of property law (following of course in the footsteps of Sir Thomas Littleton and Sir Edward Coke), he distinguished between "estates of inheritance and estates not of inheritance." By an "estate of inheritance," he referred to "the strongest and highest estate that any subject can have by these words."[80] When inheritance carries that meaning (inheritance = an immovable estate) and it is read into the articles quoted above, the provisions acquire a defensible logic, though not without confusing a civilian, since a common-law word of art was interjected, without warning or necessity, into a civil code.

A Tale of Two Translations

If the translation of the digest were the coherent work of two translators, one would expect that when any errors were made they would at least be made consistently by both men. But the faulty translation of *héritage* is not made consistently. It does not extend across the board. It is clearly the aberration of one but not the other translator. It appears in places and then disappears in others. For example, in sections immediately following the above-quoted examples, a correct translation begins to appear, and the meaning now given to *héritage* is that of an "estate" (arts. 28, 29, 33, p. 116). Incidentally, in these sections the French word *fruits* is no longer anomalously translated as "profits." Furthermore, the general style, quality, and syntax of the English text have undergone a sudden improvement. What does this sudden shift suggest?

In my view there is but one explanation for such a sudden shift. A different and obviously more accurate translator took over the work at that juncture. This "linguistic seam" is quite apparent, and so are some others. It is actually one of many junctures where the pen evidently passed from one hand to another, only to pass back again, probably in accordance with the division of labor previously agreed to between them.[81] Out of these patent differences emerges the outline of two strikingly different works, actually two translations of different quality and technical competence, which were pieced together without reconciliation, forming in effect a quilt of different cloths and colors. The different styles and clashing meanings were left in place, and there was no subsequent effort to conform or harmonize the whole. Clearly, the translators worked independently on predetermined portions of the text. They did not collaborate or critique each other, for if they had, they would have discovered the radically discontinuous treatment of repeatedly used words like *héritage* and *fruits*. Furthermore, the style and syntax of the English would not have varied so markedly from one section to the next.

Lack of collaboration, therefore, must be considered as a principal reason for the incoherence of the translation. It will be remembered that in 1808 Governor Claiborne blamed the errors of the translation on a lack of familiarity with the English language. One wonders if it was not a different issue. The translators apparently divided the text into respective parts, worked separately on those parts, conducted no cross-checking of each other's work, and did not consult with the redactors of the French text as to intended meanings. And of course one wonders why the legislative committee charged with the oversight of the civil code failed to discover these mistakes.

The (at Times) Hilarious Digest

The mistranslation of basic words like *fruits*, *héritage*, and *animaux* produced a considerable number of amusing statements. For example, one property article speaks of "profits" hanging from the tree branches and from the roots of plants, a figure that sounds not only absurd but also impossible (art. 11, p. 112). Another article entertains the notion of an "enclaved inheritance," that is, an inheritance "enclosed within the other lands" (art. 20, p. 114). The true situation was an immovable estate surrounded by other lands, but the translation insisted (at least acoustically) that an "inheritance" could be landlocked. Another article dealing with farming leases was converted into a pronouncement about a "rented" inheritance. According to the translation, the term of a praedial lease is presumed to be one year, "as that time is necessary in this territory to enable the farmer to make his crop *and to gather in all the produce of the inheritance which he has rented*."[82] Interestingly, no one sensed the anomaly (or humor) in this statement.

Inexplicably, the simple word *animaux* (animals) proved to be a *bête noir*. It was systematically translated as "cattle," a mistake that automatically altered the intended scope of the provision in question.[83] The code redactors usually stated rules applicable to all kinds of animals and rarely singled out particular species. The substitution of the word "cattle" for "animals," however, reduced the entire animal kingdom to a single bovine genus and thereby narrowed coverage obviously intended to be wider. For example, the vendor's privilege was to extend over all slaves and animals sold with an estate ("ce privilege s'etend sur les esclaves et sur les animaux vendus avec le fonds"), but in translation the privilege extended merely "to slaves and cattle sold with the estate" (art. 75, p. 470).[84] Similarly, the young born of all animals were to fall into the community of property between spouses, but now only the young born of cattle became community (art. 69, p. 338). Astonishingly, the translation managed to transform cattle into wool-bearing creatures. It allowed the usufructuary to gather cattle wool(!) for his or her own use (art. 12, p. 112). Finally, in an article intended to cover liability for the loss of any kind of animal subject to usufruct, the translator wrote, "If the usufruct consists of one head of cattle, which dies without any neglect on the part of the usufructuary, he is not bound to return another, or to pay the estimated value of the same" (art. 40, p. 118).

The Discovery of a Third Translator: Dr. William Strahan of Doctors' Commons

It is well-known that a large number of digest provisions were taken in French virtually word for word from Jean Domat's famous work *Les Loix civiles dans leur ordre naturel* (*The Civil Law in Its Natural Order*). Professor Rodolfo Batiza pointed out as many as 175 provisions of the digest (about 8 percent of the whole) were directly traceable to Domat.[85] This large-scale indebtedness to a single French author apparently tempted Davezac and Nugent to take a labor-saving shortcut. Rather than devising an original translation of the borrowed provisions, they copied directly from an old translation by Dr. William Strahan published in 1722. Comparison of the two translations reveals that at least fifty-nine articles of the digest are direct copies from Strahan (verbatim or nearly verbatim). Strahan is the source of the translation of sixteen provisions on persons (arts. 3–19, pp. 8–10), three articles on predial servitudes (arts. 15–17, p. 130), sixteen articles on possession (arts. 16–31, pp. 476–80), ten articles on transactions (arts. 1, 3, 4, 5–8, 10, 13, 14, pp. 434–36), three articles on usufruct (arts. 52, 53, 57, pp. 120–22), two articles on sales (arts. 26, 30, p. 350), four articles on compromise and arbitration (arts. 26–29, p. 444), four articles on prescription (art. 32, p. 482, paras. 2–3; art. 40, p. 482, para. 2; arts. 43 and 44, p. 484), and one article on mandate (art. 1, p. 420). Incidentally, one would have been hard-pressed to discover the existence of this borrowed translation had not Professor Batiza pointed out the exact places in which Domat's work was the source of the French text.

To appreciate the significance and scope of this borrowing we need go no further than the articles under the title "Of Possession." These are not merely clear examples of verbatim copying; instead, they also show Nugent and Davezac's uncritical acceptance of some of Strachan's most eccentric phrases. For example, in articles 21 and 22, the translators incorporated Strachan's strange expression "the knavish possessor" to translate the possessor "de mauvaise foi." Likewise, they accepted his expression "the honest and fair possessor" to translate the possessor "de bonne foi." These unusual and awkward phrases were received into Louisiana's civil law in 1808 solely due to slavish reliance upon Dr. William Strachan of Doctors' Commons.[86]

The "Translation within a Translation": Comparisons from the Title "Of Possession"

DIGEST ART. 16

Possession taken in a proper sense, is the detention of a thing which he who is master of it, or who has reason to believe that he is so, has in his own keeping or in that of another person by whom he possesses.

STRAHAN'S DOMAT PARA. 2127

Possession, taken in a proper sense, is the detention of a thing, which he who is master of it, or who has reason to believe that he is so, has in his own keeping, or in that of another person by whom he possesses.

DIGEST ART. 18

One may possess a thing not only by one's self, but also by other persons. Thus the proprietor of a house or other tenement, possesses by his tenant or by his farmer; the minor by his tutor or curator, and in general every proprietor by the persons who hold the thing in his name.

STRAHAN'S DOMAT PARA. 2135

One may possess a thing, not only by one's self, but also by other persons. Thus the proprietor of a house or other tenement, possesses by his tenant, or by his farmer . . . and in general every proprietor possesses by the persons who hold the thing in his name.

DIGEST ART. 19

Seeing the use of property is to have a thing in order to enjoy it and dispose of it, and that it is only by possession, that one can exercise this right, possession is therefore naturally linked to the property. Thus possession implies a right and a fact, the right to enjoy annexed to the right of property and the fact of the real detention of the thing, that it be in the hands of the master or of another for him.

STRAHAN'S DOMAT PARA. 2128

Seeing the use of property is to have a thing in order to enjoy it and to dispose of it, and that it is only by possession that one can exercise this right; possession therefore is naturally linked to the property. . . . Thus, possession implies a right and a fact; the right to enjoy annexed to the right of property, and the fact of the real detention of the thing, that it be in the hands of the master, or of another for him.

DIGEST ART. 20

Although the possession be naturally linked with the property, yet they may subsist separately from each other, for it often happens that the property of a thing being controverted between two persons, there is one of the two who is owned to be possessor, and it may be that it is the person who is not the right owner, and that thus the possession may be separated from the property.

STRAHAN'S DOMAT PARA. 2139

Although the possession be naturally linked with the property, and ought not to be separated from it; yet we must not confound them, so as to believe that the one cannot be without the other. For it often happens that, the property of a thing being controverted between two persons, there is only one of the two who is owned to be possessor, and it may be that it is the person who is not the right owner, and that thus the possession may be separated from the property.

DIGEST ART. 21

There are two sorts of possessors, those who possess honestly and fairly, and those who possess knavishly.

The honest and fair possessor is he who is truly master of the thing which he possesses or who has just cause to believe that he is so, although it may happen in effect that he is not; as it happens to him who buys a thing which he thinks belongs to the person whom he buys it of and yet belongs to another.

The knavish possessor is he who possesses as master, but who assumes this quality when he knows very well either that he has no title to the thing or that his title thereto is vicious and defective.

STRAHAN'S DOMAT PARA. 2137

There are two sorts of possessors, those who possess honestly and fairly, and those who possess knavishly. The honest and fair possessor is he who is truly master of the thing which he possesses, or who has just cause to believe that he is so, although it may happen in effect that he is not; as it happens to him who buys a thing which he thinks belongs to the person whom he buys it of, and yet belongs to another. The knavish possessor is he who possesses as master, but who assumes this quality when he knows very well, either that he has no title at all to it, or that his title thereto is vicious and defective.

DIGEST ART. 22

We must reckon in the number of knavish possessors not only usurpers, but also those who foreseeing that the right which they pretend to have, will be disputed and fearing lest they should be hindered from taking possession thereof, take some opportunity of getting into possession surreptitiously without the knowledge of the person from whom they expect the opposition.

STRAHAN'S DOMAT PARA. 2138

We must reckon in the number of knavish possessors, not only usurpers, but also those who, foreseeing that the right which they pretend to have will be disputed, and fearing lest they should be hindered from taking possession thereof, take some opportunity of getting into possession surreptitiously, without the knowledge of the person from whom they expect the opposition.

The discovery of this "translation within a translation" helps us understand an interesting debate between David Snyder and Rodolfo Batiza over whether the digest provisions on possession come directly from the Roman law or from French commentators like Domat and Pothier.[87] Snyder maintains that Batiza's ability to trace specific language in the digest back to these French commentators does not explain how unified concepts of possession arise in the law. The story of Strahan's borrowed translation, of which neither author was apparently aware, may throw some light upon their debate. It tends to show the importance of specific language formulations and immediate linguistic antecedents. Domat's exact words in French, as opposed to his older sources in Latin, were used to produce civil code provisions on possession in two languages, and this required two steps. First, Domat's words were borrowed by the redactors of the digest; then, they were borrowed again in their English translation by the translators. This is not to deny that Roman law was a foundational source of substantive concepts of possession, indeed was the foundation of Domat's work, but in Louisiana's codification period, Domat was specifically singled out as an approved source of law. (He received a special imprimatur in the Declaratory Act of 1806, and his work was required reading for admission to the bar.) Because he presented Roman law in a rational *ordre naturel* and wrote in a modern language understood in Louisiana, he was considered by both the Louisiana legislature and the state supreme court as the clearest avenue to the Roman law foundations.

Strahan's translation was not an obscure work in America. It was popular in the eighteenth century and a favorite lawbook of some notable American lawyers. It was found in the libraries of such luminaries as Thomas Jefferson, John Jay, John Adams, and Joseph Story.[88] Domat's rational ordering of Roman law was especially valued in early Louisiana as a conduit back to the roots of the civil law. Strahan's translation certainly brought Domat within the reach of the anglophone bench and bar. In the so-called Declaratory Act of 1806, the territorial legislature singled out Domat as an approved source of Louisiana's civil law.[89] In 1840 the Supreme Court made the French author prescribed reading for applicants to the bar. Clearly, a copy of Strahan's translation was in the hands of the Louisiana translators, but how or where they obtained it remains unclear. No copy is listed in the leading libraries that have been inventoried, though of course it may have been obtained elsewhere.[90] It is also unclear but intriguing to ask how the translators first realized that Domat was the verbatim source of the French texts under translation, for without that knowledge it is unlikely they would have consulted the Strahan translation. Based on a statement attributed to Moreau-Lislet in which he emphatically denied any involvement in the translation ("We have nothing to do with the imperfections of the translation of the Code—the French text, in which it is known that work was drawn up, leaves no doubt"), it has long been assumed that there was no contact between the translators and the jurisconsults.[91] Yet the recourse to the Strahan translation suggests that some communication must have taken place. For who else, other than Moreau-Lislet and Brown, would have known that Domat was the source of so many French texts and could have pointed out with precision the dispersed titles and sections where Strahan's translation was relevant?

Daniel Coquillette placed Strahan in the fourth generation of the jurists of Doctors' Commons, a group that "retreated" into the study of civilian doctrine for its own sake.[92] In the preface to his work, Strahan expressed the hope that his translation might have some utility in America, namely, "in the Government of the English Plantations." His goal was "to make civilian doctrines accessible in a palatable form."[93] The main readership he had in mind was common lawyers in England and America, which explains why his annotations attempted to illustrate important differences between Continental and English national law and why he interspersed common-law terms in the topical headings. It would have required clairvoyance to envision its utility in Louisiana three-quarters of a century later, yet his methods and aims were quite compatible with the needs and orientation of the English-speaking civilians in a mixed jurisdiction.

The "Surprising" Blackstone

Professor Batiza registered surprise when he discovered that Sir William Blackstone was one of the important sources of the digest: "The surprising presence of Blackstone in a civilian code . . . was perhaps a concession that had to be made to the common law." He found that Blackstone was a source in four titles of the digest: the "Preliminary Title," "Father and Child," "Master and Servant," and "Communities and Corporations."[94]

To understand the presence of Blackstone in the digest one should consider not only the great influence he exercised on the early Louisiana jurists but also the nature of the ideas borrowed from him.

The *Commentaries* was perhaps the one common-law work that Louisiana judges and lawyers regarded as indispensable.[95] It was frequently cited in court opinions and even in civil cases, and it was regarded as especially authoritative in criminal law.[96] Moreau-Lislet possessed two sets of the *Commentaries* in his library, one in English and another in French translation.[97] Judge Martin also owned a copy of Blackstone and made extensive use of it.[98] The Louisiana Supreme Court designated the *Commentaries* as examination material for admission to the bar. Michel Morin tells us that Blackstone played a similar role in Quebec in shaping its Anglo-French legal culture.[99]

Borrowings from Blackstone usually consisted of general principles of law that were of universal application and were by no means unique to the common law. John Cairns noted that "Blackstone was used when he provided a neatly turned, borrowable expression in English of a general rule embodying universal practice."[100] The digest articles laying down the canons and maxims on interpretation of the laws, for example, fit this description. Batiza and Cairns agreed that at least four canons in the "Preliminary Title" were borrowed from Blackstone.[101] These canons were not Blackstone's invention but were rooted in the natural law tradition. As Alejandro Guzmán Brito noted, they descended directly from Hugo Grotius and Samuel von Pufendorf, as Blackstone's own notes acknowledged.[102] Indeed, in treating this subject, Blackstone used only civilian citations and not one common-law reference. Borrowing universal principles from an English author like Blackstone, therefore, need not amount to a "concession to the common law," as Professor Batiza surmised, but may have been a highly convenient means of importing Continental sources in the English language. Incidentally, this particular borrowing from Blackstone would not support Professor Pascal's theory that the drafters, though copying provisions from non-Spanish sources, could be actually observing a substantive rule of Spanish law. The Blackstonian canons of interpretation were contrary to substantive Spanish law. Moreau-Lislet acknowledged that the digest repealed the provision in *Las siete partidas* (7.33.4) that forbade anyone other than the king from interpreting the laws.[103]

Blackstone was quite familiar to both the codifiers and the translators of the Digest of Orleans. As mentioned earlier, Moreau-Lislet possessed two sets of the *Commentaries* in his library, and he was familiar with it as early as 1805, when he translated Lewis Kerr's *Exposition of the Criminal Laws of the Territory of Orleans*, a book that cited Blackstone forty-five times.[104] Moreau-Lislet copied passages at length. Kerr sought from Blackstone precise definitions that differentiated related crimes from one another. For example, to go no further than the entry titled "Manslaughter," Kerr quoted Blackstone to establish (1) how manslaughter is defined, (2) how it differs from murder, (3) how it differs from excusable homicide *se defendendo*, and (4) whether murder or only manslaughter results when an involuntary killing arises during the commission of an unlawful act.[105] This reliance is impressive because it was total. Kerr's work does not directly quote any author other than Blackstone.

James Brown, considering his legal training as an American lawyer, had stronger reason and certainly more opportunity than Moreau to be familiar with Kerr's text.[106] An original reason in favor of choosing Brown as a drafter may well have been that though he was born in Kentucky and possessed of American legal training, he held an eclectic, nonchauvinistic attitude toward the two legal traditions. In his correspondence, he stated the desirability of drafting a code of mixed sources composed of civil law, Spanish ordinances, British statute and common law, and "the code of all the states," and he believed that the people of Louisiana were "prepared for a reception of a code ably compiled from these several systems."[107] Brown's ecumenical views about civil law and common law suggest that he would not have hesitated to borrow from Blackstone. Indeed, if one were to guess which of the two codifiers may have initiated recourse to Blackstone, Brown might be thought more likely than Moreau-Lislet.

Blackstone also played a central role in the lives and careers of the translators. As a criminal law specialist, Davezac developed a large criminal practice, and thus the fourth volume of the *Commentaries*, titled *Public Wrongs*, should have been his vade mecum. We saw earlier that when he obtained Nugent's acquittal in the case of *Territory v. Nugent*, Davezac attacked the indictment on the basis of Blackstone's so-called niceties.[108] As far as Nugent is concerned, he quoted Blackstone in his pamphlets and papers more than any other common-law author. He quoted Blackstone to support the claim that his detention in prison without bail was unlawful under English law.[109] He also quoted Blackstone's view that "the dearest interest of this country are its laws and its constitution; against every attack on these, there will, I hope, be always found among us the firmest spirit of resistance."[110] In testimony at his trial for libel, Nugent quoted to the jury Blackstone's definition of libel: "A libel, said I, is defined by Blackstone, a writing which upon a fair and impartial trial, shall be found to be of pernicious tendency."[111]

Judge Martin's opinion in *Territory v. Nugent* cited the *Commentaries* extensively, first as authority for the proposition that truth was not a defense to the charge of criminal libel; second, to show that Nugent's indictment was invalid in form; and third, to hold that the English precedents tending to invalidate the indictment were binding on the Superior Court in Louisiana.[112] On this last point Martin appropriated, word for word and without acknowledgment, whole passages in which Blackstone praised the virtues of stare decisis.[113]

The scholarship of Rodolfo Batiza, Thomas Tucker, and John Cairns concerning Blackstone's contribution to the digest has been most impressive, yet since these authors paid little attention to the translation as a whole, a more basic and pervasive sign of his influence may have been overlooked.[114] It has not been previously noticed that the translators embedded Blackstone's terminology in certain parts of the translation. The translators introduced a number of common-law terms of art (e.g., "inheritance," "profits," "obligor/obligee") that, in my opinion, come straight from Blackstone. These words were repeatedly used (though not always correctly) for the benefit of an anglophone bench and bar. To be sure, legal terms like these were not unique to Blackstone. They were commonly used by many writers before him, including Lord Coke and Littleton. Nevertheless, it is reasonable to speculate here that the immediate inspiration came from Blackstone. As I have noted earlier, both the translators and codifiers read and relied heavily upon Blackstone in their own careers and writings. The *Commentaries* was widely distributed in Louisiana's legal libraries, frequently cited in court, and carried prestige that other common-law authorities never attained. And these same factors could explain why it was also a word-for-word source of provisions in four different titles of the digest.

An Untethered Freedom:
Underinclusive and Overinclusive Translation

Some texts drafted in French by Moreau-Lislet and Brown were *incompletely translated* or, put another way, only partially translated. At the same time, other texts were *overtranslated* in the sense that the English version went quite beyond the French. The point is that at times the translation was underinclusive and therefore an incomplete transcription, while at other times it was overinclusive when it contained unsolicited paraphrases and interpolations.

Incompleteness of translation was the most frequent and recurrent type of error detected by Professor Joseph Dainow in his *1972 Compiled Edition of the Civil Codes of Louisiana*. Sometimes the translators ignored words, phrases, and even entire sentences in the French draft. A comprehensive count of this phenomenon has not been made, but it easily involves more than one hundred instances. It will suffice to mention below a few examples:

—In a provision on subrogated debts, there is no translation of a sentence that permits subrogation to take place without seeking the creditor's approval (art. 150, p. 290, para. 2).
—In a provision dealing with rights of accession to movable property, an important phrase ("si les matières peuvent être separées") was not translated, though the part that *was* translated is unintelligible without the part omitted (art. 27, p. 108).[115]
—A provision on the forced sale and seizure of property omitted this sentence: "But immovables and slaves cannot be seized until after the discussion of the movables" (art. 2, p. 490).
—A provision stating that partitions in the prescribed form are final between the parties omitted the following sentence: "Any other partition can only be provisional" (art. 68, p. 70).[116]

It would be natural at first glance to attribute such gaps or omissions to haste or inattention, but this excuse cannot explain away the contrasting phenomenon of overtranslation. Additions and interpolations are by nature intentional departures from the original. They are unlikely to be the result of haste or negligence, and in any event the cumulative gloss on the original is too massive and broadly distributed to be unintentional.[117] The gloss signals that the translators did not feel literally or rigidly tied down by the French texts. The following are illustrations:

—A provision dealing with the remedy of redhibition added fourteen words ("from the importance more or less of the qualities which may have been announced") that have no counterpart in the French text (art. 81, p. 360).
—A provision regarding the acceptance of a succession formed

a single sentence in French (art. 76 below), but the translation proved twice that length and introduced a second paragraph that has no counterpart in the French version:

ART. 76, P. 162

The acceptance is simple when the heir has manifested his intention to be heir, without having recourse to the benefit of the inventory. When he has had recourse to that mode, the acceptation is then called with the benefit of an inventory.

ART. 76, P. 163

L'acceptation est pure et simple, lorsque l'hérétier a témoigné sa volonté d'être hérétier, sans avoir recours au bénéfice d'inventaire.

—A provision on "collation of goods" had two paragraphs in French, but when translated the second paragraph was entirely omitted. Therefore, as enacted, the provision consisted of two paragraphs in French and one paragraph in English. The missing paragraph, however, was in fact translated but showed up in another place. It was tacked onto the *next* succeeding article, so that this article now appeared as two (logically unconnected) paragraphs in English set against a single paragraph in French.[118]

CODA

The story of the lost translators of 1808 is intimately connected to the birth of Louisiana civil law *in English* and therefore to its remarkable survival in Louisiana for more than two centuries. The English version proved to be increasingly important to the life of the law after the sudden collapse of the French language during the nineteenth century. Louisiana did little to defend and retain the French language, and the state emerged practically unilingual in the twentieth century. It grew increasingly difficult to access that law in the French language, and if the civil law implanted in 1808 was to survive in the long run, it would survive in the English language. In that sense, Louisiana civil law has lived off of translations, and the nature of its civil law has been subliminally shaped by the decisions of translators. Nugent and Davezac were the shapers of a particular kind of civil law, one that accommodated and anticipated the understanding of a common-law audience.

In paging through the translation, we have not definitively established which parts were translated by Davezac and which parts by Nugent, but it has been shown that there are in fact two independent parts that have been stitched together. The stylistic and conceptual differences between the two are glaring; the linguistic seams are apparent. The translation is not a seamless cloth but something like a patchwork quilt.

Nugent and Davezac invented important neologisms, such as the obligor/obligee distinction in the field of obligations, and they also borrowed, nearly verbatim, a large amount of material from an old translation of

Domat by William Strahan. Furthermore, in numerous places, rather than attempt a literal translation, Nugent and Davezac inserted equivalent common-law concepts or legal terms that they thought would resonate with the bench and bar of early Louisiana. This feature of the translation demonstrated that the primary audience the translators held in mind was the recently arrived and untutored anglophone bench and bar. In light of that aim and audience, English served as something more than simply the target language; it was also the medium of another legal culture and served a legal profession primarily trained, educated, and inured to the common law.

This represented a consequential step in the birth of a distinct kind of civil law in Louisiana, for the anglicized translation enabled an immediate reception of corresponding common-law ideas. It ensured that the civil law arrived on the scene in some degree preemptively mixed with common-law terms. It may seem curious, however, that the common-law ideas were expressed exclusively in one language (English) and were not found in the other (French) and that the English text was destined for a distinct readership with its own cultural understandings.

In closing, I submit that the lost translators of 1808 left to posterity a fascinating object: a true artifact of Louisiana's mixed-jurisdiction experience and a mirror of the historical conditions that shaped it.

APPENDIX

Selected Writings of Henry Paul Nugent and Auguste Valentin Geneviève Davezac de Castera

1. Lewis Kerr's Address to the Jury at
Nugent's Trial for Libel and Contempt (1808)
From *Echo du Commerce*, New Orleans, September 28, 1808

Au Rédacteur de l'Echo du Commerce
Monsieur,
Me proposant de publier mon procès dans une brochure, j'avais prié mon Avocat M. Kerr de me donner par écrit le discours qù'il avait prononcé à cette occasion.

Je me vois dans la nécessité d'abandonner le projet de publier cet écrit, par la raison que je n'ai pu obtenir la décision de la cour sur la motion de M. Workmann [*sic*], pour faire casser toute la procédure comme étant illégal. Cette décision était par écrit, et le juge Mathews en a donné lecture. Je me promettais bien de prouver qu'elle était contraire aux lois et à la raison, mais les juges, en la supprimant, m'en ont ôté les moyens. Comme le discours de M. Kerr est très intéressant, je vous le remets pour que vous l'insériez dans votre Gazette, si vous le jugez à propos:

Je suis, Monsieur, & c
H. P. Nugent

M. Kerr; Messieurs du Jury;

Je ne suis nullement porté à défendre ni à justifier l'abus de ce privilège sacré qui assûre au citoyen la liberté de donner publicité à son vertueux ressentiment des injures qu'il pourrait avoir souffertes. La liberté de la presse est d'autant plus essentielle sous un gouvernement tel qu'on prétend qu'est celui des E.U., qu'elle est la clef qui forme l'arche politique de la constitution, le vrai niveleur de la condition humaine, le rempart sans lequel la liberté civile ne pourrait se défendre un seul jour contre la tyrannie des gens en place d'un côté, et du caprice du peuple de l'autre. Pour ces raisons je révère tellement la liberté de la presse, que je suis l'ennemi déclaré de tout ce qui tend à la détruire ou à la corrompre, soit par le bras armé du glaive du pouvoir dominant, ou par les effets funestes de ces principes de sa propre destruction que renferme cette liberté, et qui la portent à la licence. Tels sont mes sentimens dans la vie privée, et à Dieu ne plaise que je ne m'en écarte jamais au barreau. Jamais je n'y ai entrepris la défense d'un calomniateur, et j'espère qu'on ne me verra jamais plaider la cause de la méchanceté devant le tribunal ou ailleurs.

La calomnie est un crime des plus odieux, et l'argent ne me tentera jamais à prêter mon secours pour détourner le glaive vengeur de la justice, de la tête du méchant dont la malice aurait versé le poison le plus mortel dans la coupe de l'innocence. Mais dans la cause actuelle, malgré toutes les clameurs que quelques individus ont excitées contre le défendant, je ne vois en lui rien qui caractérise le calomniateur. M. Nugent est connu pour avoir publié plusieurs écrits, mais il ne s'agit ici que du seul écrit sur lequel il est accusé de libelle. Je ne doute pas qu'il ne soit prêt à se défendre sur tout ce qu'il a pu écrire, avec la même confiance qui le rassûre au sujet de l'accusation sur laquelle vous allez, Messieurs, le juger. Je vous prie seulement de ne pas confondre ses autres écrits, avec celui dont on se plaint dans l'acte d'accusation; car la seule question soumise à la délibération des Juges et du Jury, ou sujette à discussion du barreau, c'est de savoir si l'écrit cité dans l'acte d'accusation est libelle.

Avant de discuter cette question, je dois vous prévenir, Messieurs, que le défendant et ses défenseurs ont à lutter contre bien des difficultés resultant de l'avantage qu'a pris le procureur-général en poursuivant le défendant, non pas par Bill trouvé par le grand Jury, mais par Information, c'est-à-dire de son chef. Je ne puis croire qu'un grand Jury aurait trouvé Bill dans cette affaire, à moins qu'on a trié un exprès pour cette occasion, comme il n'arrive que trop souvent qu'on trie un grand Jury pour faire réussir quelque projet politique, et pour opprimer les citoyens par le ministère de ceux à qui leur sûreté est commise. Un sage grand Jury n'eût fait que rire des expressions qui ne prouvent que la colère où était celui qui s'en est servie, et il vous eut épàrgné, Messieurs, la peine de vous occuper de cette affaire. Un Bill trouvé par le grand Jury a d'autant plus de poids qu'il énonce l'opinion qu'à portée sur un fait un grand nombre des citoyens les plus respectables, après l'avoir mûrement considéré. Mais une information ne vient que du seul procureur–général; et elle ne mérite aucune considération indépendamment des preuves au soutien. Lorsque l'accusateur public poursuit un citoyen par une voie aussi extraordinaire, il faut soupçonner, ou plutôt il semble avouer qu'il a été réduit à cet expedient, par la persuasion où il était que le grand Jury n'aurait pas trouvé matière à accusation.

Il est si évident que tout concourt à faire préférer à un accusateur de poursuivre par Bill, qu'il y a y lieu de croire que le procureur-général ne s'en est dispensé que dans le désespoir d'obtenir la sanction du grand Jury.

Mais ce n'est pas là le seul désavantage où le defendant se voit réduit par cette procédure. On le poursuit criminellement pour un fait qui ne devait naturellement donner lieu qu'à une action civile; car il n'est pas accusé d'avoir rien écrit de séditieux, ni qui pût nuire au public. Il n'est accusé que d'avoir publié un libelle contre un particulier qui ne jouit pas de la plus haute considération dans la société, bien qu'il soit à-la-fois maître de poste et juge-de-paix. Si M. Cenas a cru que M. Nugent l'a calomnié dans son écrit, le moyen de défendre sa réputation et de punir son calomniateur était de lui intenter un procés civil dans lequel le defendant eut eu la faculté de prouver la vérité des assertions contenues dans l'écrit qu'on pretend être un libelle. Et l'examen des faits, et la connaisance de tout ce qui a donné lieu à cet écrit, aurait fait voir si c'est un libelle, ou si c'est un invective contre les torts de l'oppresseur. Mais M. Cenas avait peut-être ses raisons pout éviter l'investigation de la vérité, et il a peut-être montré sa sagesse en poursuivant le défendant criminellement.

2. Nugent Defends the Liberty of the Press

From H. P. Nugent, *An Account of the Territory of Orleans against Thierry & Nugent for Libels and Contempt of Court, with an Account of Nugent's Trial on an Indictment for a Libel* (Philadelphia, 1810), 1, 37–47.

When a citizen is persuaded that he has been oppressed, and that the forms of law have been resorted to, merely to cloak the injustice of wicked men, who sought to ruin him, he cannot render a more acceptable service to the community, than by exposing the depravity of those who dare to pervert the administration of justice into an instrument of private vengeance.

The attempts that have been made to prevent my appealing to the public, sufficiently prove that my prosecutors are conscious that a fair exposition of facts will consign them to infamy. To stifle the voice of truth, they have forced me to give security for the peace, and for my good behaviour, during six months, on account of writings which they term libellous, but which I trust, to every man of sense will appear to have been dictated by a spirit of justice, and to be highly conducive to the public good, inasmuch as they expose villains to the scorn and execration of all who have any sense of virtue, any abhorrence of injustice.

It is with a view, at once to vindicate the freedom of the press, that terror of oppressors, and to defend my honour, that I have resolved to publish an account of the proceedings had against Mr. Theirry and me, on charges of libel and contempt of court. If, in defending my constitutional rights, and my reputation, I am forced to make the malice of my enemies recoil on themselves, those who have driven me to this necessity, can have no right to complain of the consequences of their own justice. . . .

Never surely did a judge [Judge Martin] behave more scandalously on a trial. The reason assigned by judge Martin why the truth could not be given in evidence, was that judge Lewis could not be tried without presentment or indictment, that being an article locked up in the tabernacle of the constitution, which even the legislature could not touch. I dexterously took advantage of this, and having brought him explicitly to declare that without presentment or indictment a man could not be tried for a libel: "Can it then, said I, be a crime in me to have expressed my detestation of judges who, to oppress me, have violated the constitution? The records of this court attest that I have been tried, convicted, and imprisoned for a libel, on information; and I think it my duty to expose judges who, either through gross ignorance or the most daring iniquity, deprived a citizen of his most sacred right. The court observes that I ought to have complained to the grand jury, or to the legislature. I have done both. In the case of Mr. Workman I accused the judge on affidavit, and in a letter I observed to the grand jury that they could not, consistently with their oath, avoid presenting the judge, unless they presented me for perjury. To the legislature

I presented a memorial on the oppression of judges of which I had been the victim. It was shuffled out of the house without having been read, and when Mr. Hughes called for the reading of it, no one could tell what had become of it. What resource was then left to me, but an appeal to the protecting authority of public opinion, to which all other authorities are subordinate?"

The whole court saw judge Martin was confounded. He made no reply.

The reason assigned for not admitting the truth to be given evidence, was a palpable absurdity; for if to prove a fact against a man, is to put him on his trial contrary to the constitution, how can evidence of the truth be admitted in a civil action?

Some time after the usual hour for adjourning the court, Mr. Holmes observed that he found himself exhausted, that being young at the bar and young in years, he was unused to such exertions as he had so ineffectually made, and therefore he requested the court might adjourn, were it only for an hour, before he addressed the jury. On his request being refused, I spoke to judge Martin to this purport: "You have forced me to trial without the least notice, though you had clearly given me and my counsel to understand that I was not to be tried this day. You have prejudged my cause and excited prejudice against me, so as to leave me no hope of a fair trial. You have bound me over to my good behavior, on account of a publication which, of your own authority, you declared to be a libel, though nothing had been legally proved against me. The grand jury accused you, said the judge. The law, replied I, still presumed me innocent, and you have not only bound me over to my good behaviour, openly declaring me a notorious libeler, but you have constantly spoken of me as such this day. It is evident that you have prejudged my cause, and deprived me of a fair trial.

I don't know, said judge Martin, that I ought to notice what is said by a man in your situation. I replied—I am on my trial; I say but what I have right, what you have compelled me to say, and what you cannot deny. Here Mr. Davezac whispered me to sit down.

Mr. Davezac addressed the jury in French, and Mr. Holmes followed him in English. I then rose and observed to the jury that from the unfairness with which I had been forced to trial, without any notice, I could not but suspect that the prosecutors had great reliance on the predisposition of the jury towards me; that when I determined to inveigh against the conduct of judge Lewis, I was well aware that I exposed myself to persecution, and was less anxious to avoid it, than to prove to the public that I had acted as became a man of integrity, and that by my conduct I had deserved my own esteem and that of my fellow-citizens. I maintained my right to make known to the public the malversations of judges, who, but for men of my disposition, might become tyrants of impunity. The judge who presides at this trial, has declared to you, said I, that no man can be tried for a libel without presentment or indictment. Had I not then a right to inveigh against judges who had oppressed me?—Must they not be wicked men, if they knowingly violated the constitution; or contemptible, if they acted through ignorance? I am told that I had no right to publish my complaints; that I should have laid them before the proper authority. Of what use then is the liberty of the press, if all grievances can be redressed without it? That the proper authorities will neglect their duty, I know by experience; for if they had attended to my complaints, I should not have brought them before the public. I observed that I had never been of any party, and that no school-boy concerned himself less than I did about the administration of government; but that I could not, with indifference, behold flagrant injustice, and a scandalous disregard of decency in judges; that I was accused of having libeled judge Lewis in his official capacity, as if his official capacity set him above censure, whereas it was only in that capacity that he could do such injury to society, as to become a proper object of the animadversion of the press. I maintained that judges ought, above all public functionaries, to be subject to the just censure of the public, as that alone could prevent their rendering themselves absolute. To show how essentially social happiness depends on the administration of justice, and consequently that it is every man's concern, I read the following passage from Mr. Hopkinson's speech on the trial of judge Chase.

"The pure and upright administration of justice is of the utmost importance to any people. The other movements of government are not of such universal concern. Who shall be president, or what treaties or general statutes shall be made, occupied the attention of a few busy politicians; but these things touch not, or but seldom, the private interests and happiness of the great mass of the community. But the settlement of private controversies, the administration of law between man and man, the distribution of justice and right to the citizen, in his private business and concern, comes to every man's door, and is essential to every man's prosperity and happiness."

A libel, said I, is defined by Blackstone, a writing which upon a fair and impartial trial, shall be found to be of pernicious tendency. But where is the pernicious tendency of my writings, provided they be true; and what man of candour can pretend to believe them to be false, when I offer to prove the truth of all I have asserted, and the court will not suffer my witnesses to be heard? If what I have said of judge Lewis, however true, be no way to his discredit, where is the pernicious tendency? If what I have said of him, must, if true, bring him into *contempt, hatred, infamy,* and *disgrace,* what reproach is it to me to have made a moral cause produce its effect? Contempt, hatred, infamy, and disgrace, ought to attend a judge who behaves as I am ready to prove judge Lewis has done; and if, by publishing the truth of him, I have brought him to contempt, hatred, infamy, and disgrace, I return thanks to the Almighty for having given me the virtue to do it. The conduct I have exposed, must indeed have a pernicious tendency, and would be destructive of all morality, social order and government, if no man durst inveigh against it.

I observed to the jury that as the judge had frequently alluded to a hand-bill which formed no part of the indictment, to counteract the effect the judge's remarks might otherwise have on them, I would contend that the reasoning in that hand-bill could be attacked only by obloquy or by indictments, but was proof against argument; and since the judge was so confident that I was the author of the hand-bill I would avail myself of what was in it to my purpose and read it in my defence. And I read and enlarged on a considerable part of it; beginning with the contrast between the dictum of lord Mansfield as applied to useful truth, and the solicitude of the President of the United States *to preserve in their full energy the salutary provisions in behalf of the liberty of the press.*

In support, not only of the legality, but of the beneficial tendency of my libel, I read the following passages from De Lolme on the British constitution, article liberty of the press.

"If the citizens of Geneva have maintained their liberty better than the people have been able to do in the other republics of Switzerland, I believe it may be ascribed to the ample liberty they have of making public remonstrances to their magistrates. These have been still more useful to the citizens in preventing abuses, than in remedying them."

On this I observed that though I had suffered much molestation and pecuniary loss, I had the consolation to think that by my libels, which were the more *atrocious* as they were true, I had prevented many abuses.

"We may reckon, then, as a new and very great advantage of the laws of England, the liberty which they give to the people to examine and censure the conduct of government, and of all those who administer any branch thereof. Not only do they secure every individual the right of presenting petitions, either to the king or to the parliament, but they also give him that of bringing his complaints, and all his observations whatever, before the tribunal of the public, through the medium of the press. A right to be dreaded by those who govern, and which constantly dispelling the cloud of majesty in which they envelope themselves, brings them back to the level of other men, and strikes at the very principle of their authority. And it is in this very publicity of everything, that consists the power which we have observed to be so necessary to assist the inevitable imperfection of laws, and which restrains in due bounds all those who have any share of authority."

From this passage, I contended that I had not abused the liberty of the press, in libeling judge Lewis in his official capacity, if my libel advanced nothing but the truth; and if truth would justify the libel, and I was hindered from producing my witnesses, the truth must be taken for granted, in opposition to the opinion expressed by judge Martin, that I might have complained of judge Lewis to the proper authorities, but that government could pay no regard to newspaper publications or hand-bills, I read from De Lolme these words: "Today a citizen, by the publicity and force of his complaints, opens the eyes of the nation; tomorrow a member of the legislature proposes a law to restrain the abuse of authority."

I read another passage from De Lolme, as exactly describing the situation in which I was placed by those who pretended they were prosecuting me through a regard for the public good.

"The last resource of him who wishes to render himself absolute, is to employ the means that the law affords of calling to his aid the public force; and if the law has not provided against every possible abuse, he will take advantage of any omission, to cover his injustice; he will drive on to the attainment of his private ends, while his constant theme of declamation is the public good; and he will destroy the defenders of the law, under the formalities which the law has prescribed."

It is, said I, for having defended the laws, that an attempt is now made to oppress me, and it is currently reported in town, that I am to be condemned to two years imprisonment. But I have the approbation of my own conscience, and I disregard what evils man can bring on me. I glory in what I have written, conscious that I was actuated by a love of truth and justice, animated by a resolution not tamely to endure oppression. I am proud to reflect that I have evinced that there is in me something of the spirit of a Sydney and a Russel.

The attorney-general made no reply to my counsel, but appeared, during the whole trial, to be confident of the discernment of Blaise Cenas, in his choice of a jury.

Judge Martin delivered a charge, in which he constantly pleaded against me, and endeavored to work on the passions of the jury, by descanting on topics foreign from the case before him; for in his charge he even spoke for the second time of striking a judge. He said I might have complained of judge Lewis to the legislature, and might have given to each member a printed copy of my charges; but that I had no right to distribute them in taverns to the common people, that that was the way to excite sedition. He observed that if judge Lewis had acted wrong in the affair of the Bayou bridge, he might be sued for damages, or he might be indicted or impeached, if gentlemen would accuse him on oath; but that government could take no notice of hand-bills or news-paper publications. Judge Lewis, he said, had earnestly desired him to suffer, if possible, the truth to be given in evidence; and he had for somedays endeavoured to find in his books whether, by any means, the law would allow it; but that he was convinced, from his researches, that it required a legislative act to admit the truth to be given in evidence; that he could not undertake to try judge Lewis; for, that no man could be tried without a presentment or indictment, was a principle locked up in the tabernacle of the constitution, which even the legislature could not touch (and he had just admitted that a legislative act could allow the truth to be given in evidence, which he contended was trying a man). He said he was persuaded that if the truth could be admitted, it would appear that there was no truth in what I had published against judge Lewis. Legal remedies, said he, can be had against a judge, as well as against any other citizen; but is a man to be suffered to destroy his reputation, or to strike him? It is true, said he, the constitution secures the liberty of the press, but it likewise secures the liberty of keeping arms; now, as the liberty of keeping arms is not the liberty of killing or maiming whom we please, so is not the liberty of the press, the liberty of publishing libels.

After having spoken some time to this effect, repeating all he had said during the trial, the judge told the jury that they had to consider whether the publication set forth in the indictment, tended to promote public good, or to excite sedition.

No proof had been given of any hand-bill distributed in the taverns or to the common people; and judge Martin, forgetting his province, here became my accuser as to a fact, of which he had neither personal knowledge, nor legal proof. From the face of the writing indicted, it appeared that it was not intended for the common people; for the situation of judge Lewis, when trying a man for his life, after he had spent the whole night in celebrating orgies, was most aptly described in the words of Horace, without a translation. If I had written for the common people, I would have told them that the meaning of the Latin was, that his body loaded with the night's debauch, bore down the faculties of his soul, and cast on the ground that particle of the divine mind which distinguishes man from the brute creation.

It was for the second time during the trial, that judge Martin compared the liberty of the press to the right of keeping arms, and argued that as the one was not the liberty of killing or maiming, neither was the other that of publishing libels.

This pitiful sophistry was doubtless a most convincing argument to an ignorant jury; but men of sense will see in it a palpable proof of the disingenuousness of the judge. By merely keeping arms in my house, I actually exercise, even while I sleep, the right secured by the 4th article in amendment; but to exercise the freedom of speech or of the press, I must speak or publish. Therefore there is here no analogy between these two provisions, unless judge Martin will contend that as a man is a libeller for having used the constitutional liberty of the press, so is he an offender if he avails himself of the constitutional liberty of keeping arms. The conclusion in the latter case, is not more absurd than in the former. If the constitution does not give us a right to kill whom we please, it does not follow that all killing is a crime; and if it does not give us the liberty of publishing libels, neither is it to be inferred that every writing tending to render a judge infamous, is a libel. Horace and Pope contend that it is as justifiable to defend morality, by attacking villains by writing, as it is to defend one's person or one's country with arms—judge Martin wished to persuade the jury that as arms may be sometimes unlawfully used, so to wound a man through the press, must be always unlawful. It is a common artifice with imposters, to make a self-evident proposition to serve as an entering wedge for the admission of an absurdity; and, with ignorant men this stratagem is generally successful.

Judge Martin did not compare the liberty of the press to the use made of a gun, but to the right of keeping a gun; as if by the liberty of the press, the constitution intended only to secure the right of having presses in our houses. As he who has shot a man, is allowed to prove that he has shot him justly, so ought he, who has endeavoured to render a judge infamous, to be permitted to show, if he can, that he has acted no less meritoriously than he who kills in battle the enemy of his country. I am persuaded that never was the liberty of the press used more conscientiously, or for a more laudable purpose, than it was by me in those writings that have been called libels; and hence judge Martin, having no candid argument to urge against me, was forced, in defence of his righteous compeer, to attack me with sophisms still more disgraceful to the judge who used them than to the stupid jury who were the dupes of such flimsy artifice.

The jury having retired, soon returned with a verdict of guilty.

Mr. Holmes moved for a new trial, and a day was fixed to hear argument on his motion.

The attorney-general moved that I should be instantly committed to prison—a place for which, he said, a wretch like me seemed to have been born; and he added, that he had refrained from invective until the verdict of a respectable jury had authorized him to speak of me as every good citizen thought. I afterwards found that these words had excited against the attorney-general the contempt of the audience; and several gentlemen have assured me they were surprised at my silence. At any time, I should despise the base malignity of that miscreant whose turpitude is on record; but at that moment he appeared utterly beneath my notice, when I was raised in my own esteem, by reflecting that I had the honour to share the fate of many worthy men who, for their efforts in the cause of truth and justice, had been rewarded with a similar verdict, by a jury as respectable as mine, packed to assassinate them with the formalities of law.

Judge Martin replied to the attorney-general that the court had no power to commit me, but he required new security. My counsel observed that I was still under recognisance, and I added that when found guilty on an information, no additional security had been required of me; and that I would rather go to jail, than call on gentlemen so frequently to be my bail. Judge Martin persisted in requiring security, and I went to jail.

On Friday, my counsel urged several grounds for a new trial, one of which was that some of the jurors were not house keepers, as the law required that such only should serve. I objected to the jury on the ground that the sheriff was my inveterate enemy, and that I had against him an action of false imprisonment. Judge Martin said he believed, but was not certain, that our objections to the jury were made too late. I trust, sir, said I, that I have not been brought before this court to be circumvented and entrapped. According to Blackstone, my challenge to the array is as valid now as it would have been before trial. . . .

3. Nugent's Affidavit in the Account
From Nugent, *An Account of the Territory of Orleans against Thierry & Nugent*, 31–32.

H. P Nugent makes oath on the Holy Evangelists, and says that all the facts stated in a hand-bill published by him, for which hand-bill he is indicted, relative to orgies at La Fourche, he firmly believed to be true when he published the same, and still does believe that they are true. And he declares that he firmly believes that the said facts can be proved by the testimony of the following persons, to wit:—Mr. Cadet Bayor, the tavern keeper, Madam Bayor, Messrs, Hopkins, C. Baldwin. J. Baldwin, Davezac, Hennen, counselors at law, Elijas Fromantin [sic], esquire, clerk of the House of Representatives and counsellor at law, Mr. Miers, the clerk of the court, sheriff Walkins, and the whole jury who acquitted the man alluded to. And this deponent further declares that he firmly believes that by the testimony of Messrs. Allard, Dorville, Fortin, and Blanque, he can convict judge Lewis of falsehood, in the following assertion, in his opinion delivered in court in writing:—"The order of injunction was predicated upon a conviction that the changing the site of the bridge was solely the act of the city council."

And this deponent further declares that he firmly believes, that by the testimony of several gentleman of the bar and others, he can convict judge

Lewis of falsehood, and of the most base and cruel oppression, in the case of the expulsion of Mr. Workman from the bar.

And this deponent further declares that the case of Mr. Dormenon has ever appeared to him one of the most horrid outrages on justice ever committed in a country where there existed not a civil war, even when admitting Mr. Dormenon to have committed what he is charged with, by men who, from their own testimony, appear to this deponent to be senseless and malignant calumniators. And he further declares that from the testimony published by Daudet, declaring that the said publication was authorized by the court, and the evident intent of which publication appears to this deponent to have been to blacken the character of Mr. Dormenon, it appears most manifest to this deponent that the said Dormenon was in St. Domingo a man as free from reproach as any person in the island. And deponent firmly believes that, according to our laws, the persons concerned in bringing Mr. Dormenon to trial, would be convicted of conspiracy, if they appeared to the jury to be men of sound mind; and he further believes that were Mr. Dormenon to bring against them a civil action, he would recover heavy and vindictive damages.

H. P. Nugent, *New Orleans*, sworn before me this 1st day of June, 1810
Charles Trudeau, Recorder

4. Auguste Davezac's Campaign Speech at Trenton, New Jersey
Young Hickory Banner, September 9, 1844, New York

Great Mass Meeting at Trenton. The State Convention at Trenton, on the fifth instant, was the largest political assemblage ever seen in the State of New Jersey. About two thousand persons, including the Empire Club, went from the city of New York. The delegation of Southern Democrats, numbering some two hundred, with appropriate badges and banners, went in the six o'clock train. Nearly every Southern State, as well as Texas, was represented. Speeches were made by Evan Evans, Esq., the president of the convention; John M. Reid, of Philadelphia; Capt. Robert F. Stockton, U.S.N.; Maj. Auguste Davezac of New York; and Hon. John McKeon, of New York. The characteristic speech of Maj. Davezac will be read with interest, and it is only one for which we can find sufficient space.

Maj. D. being loudly called for, came forward and spoke as follows:—

Fellow Democrats: My embarrassment on rising and addressing such an assembly, and superadded to the consciousness of fixing on myself, by that act, your attention, which has just been riveted on a man who is your own neighbor, your friend, and, for those and many other reasons, entitled fully to the applause which has been bestowed upon him publicly and privately, it is almost too much for me. Fellow-Democrats, this is entwined by a cord of associations; the very ground on which I stand is classic; a voice from it rushes on the wind, and eloquently teaches an awful lesson of war and peace: the very land, the very city, in which this immense multitude is convened, teaches us that in November next, that success must be won by those who assail; and that fortune, whom the ancients reverenced under the female form, must, like the softer sex, be won warmly—aye, fiercely too. (Laughter.) In peace, it teaches also that you must assail, as well as in war, in order to triumph; it teaches the opposing sides the tactics of 1840; that the sword once in hand, we are to prefer the policy of Martius of that of Fabius—to drop low the shield, wave high the sword, and rush upon the foe, crying out, "Polk and Dallas for ever." (Applause.) Although not accustomed to address audiences, yet I do so now with readiness- and with the more that it gives me a pride to proclaim myself, after forty-five years, a member of the same cause, and a son of the same vine and laurel land which was the first ally of young America. But I will not boast of this in New Jersey; you are the sons of Lafayette and Rochambault [sic]. No, I have not got clear of my native accent, nor do I wish—and I'll tell you why. As long as I have it, but few words are necessary to show that I am no Englishman. (Great cheering.) Fellow-citizens, I feel fatigued and tired, but I have been accustomed, since the Baltimore convention, to run four-mile heats in a day, and you have re-kindled my ardor at the light of your torches. I have no studied harangue to make—I am no sluggish canal, where water steals sluggishly and slowly along. I am the Mohawk, or your own lovely river, daring and bounding from rock to rock. I am no hack, but the wild horse of the prairie. I stick my spurs into the mad animal who takes me as his guide. I have been asked if I was prepared to address you. Prepared? Ah, fellow-citizens, a long experience has taught me that it is not upon the hustings that enthusiasm depends; it rises from the people toward the hustings—like the summer squalls that the mariner sees at sea, when after the lightning as often ascends from the surface of the globe to the sky, as it descends from the heaven to earth. It is the enthusiasm of the audience that reaches the auditors, and what he receives he only gives back. (Cheers.) When I stand before the people, the spirit I feel is not mine—I receive it from them, and to them I send it back. (Applause.) Fellow-citizens, the great question now before us is, shall we remain as we are, or shall we be dictated to by Lord Aberdeen and a British Parliament. (Cries of No! no!!) Shall we, at their bidding, refuse our sympathies to a people of kindred blood—to a people who won their freedom under Houston at the battle of San Jacinto. (Applause, and three cheers for Houston.) And shall the American eagle lower her wings because Lord Aberdeen says he will let loose the British Lion to claw her? When we were yet an infant in the cradle, the young Hercules arose in his might, strangled the monster, and sent it again across the ocean (applause); and shall we now be dictated to by being threatened with British animals? Ah, we had one just now addressing us, who is a fair sample of the men who command our navy. (Cheers.) What you did once we can do again. You overthrew at New Orleans sixteen thousand of the veterans of Wellington, who came to conquer us, they said (applause); but what did they conquer? They could not conquer even a grave for their dead, but had to come, and tamely as men could do, and ask permission to bury their dead. The wretches! Ah, if it were an owl, or even a coon (loud laughter), he had to contend against, instead of that bird whose gaze confronts the sun, they might have some chance to send their British leopards against us; but we will send him back with stripes more numerous and lasting than nature has put upon his ribs. (Laughter and cheering.) The Federalists tell us that we have land enough. The immortal Thos. Jefferson, by his wisdom and foresight, procured for the American people a wider empire than ever the Macedonian conqueror acquired in his wild career—more productive of countless wealth than ever Caesar wrested from the Gauls. (Continued cheering.) You never can please these Federalists unless you cower before England. They tell us we have no generals to command in case we went to war. Is not Old Hickory alive? (Great cheering.) Why does that flag now wave with Polk and Dallas inscribed upon it? Why was planted that tall hickory pole? Not to grow, but as an emblem of the cause it represents, which spreads over the land its luxuriant foliage—a type of him, the man of Hermitage, who if he mounted his horse tomorrow, and says "Go!" one hundred thousand Americans are up at the word. Land enough!—land enough! Make way, I say, for the young American Buffalo—he has not yet got land enough: he wants more land as his cool shelter in summer—he wants more land for his beautiful pasture grounds. I tell you, we will give him Oregon for his summer shade, and the region of Texas as his winter pasture. (Applause.) Like all of his race, he wants salt, too. Well, he shall have the use of two oceans—the mighty Pacific and the turbulent Atlantic shall be his; for I tell you that the day is not far distant, when with one leap he shall bound across the puny lakes that separate Canada from America, and pitch right into the other side (loud cheering), and take possession of that land, which, from the day it was dyed with blood of Montgomery, was American. He shall not stop his career until he slakes his heart in the frozen ocean. (Cheers.) Ah! Fellow citizens, I have glad tidings to impart. From the eyening that followed the Baltimore convention, after the nomination which so happily terminated—that terrible day which poured torrents of gladness on the hearts of Federalists—I shall never forget it. I see one that partook of my trouble—that gentleman with the white hat—it was a terrible sight. The waters were agitated; the billows tossed their mad-heads on high; the old ship of the United States had well high sprained her cable. The Whigs cried out, "It will break!" "No!" I said—"it is of American iron; it is forged by the people in the furnace of freedom; they hammered it with the arms, and it will weather the storm." It did so; and that old cable is so taught [sic] that the grand ship may coil her anchor in safety at the Rio del Norte and ride in safety on the frozen ocean. (Cheering.) Ah, fellow-citizens, at that were the foes of our institutions striving to divide the Union—let them try to divide it if they can. There is a principle of adhesion in this Union, which will show that whoever attempts to divide it will be crushed in that attempt. Oh, fellow-citizens, at that moment, when the tempest raged, the Democracy came, and like that herd which Jupiter called into his service, it spread its wings at the deliberation, and hove forth to the world the names of Polk and Dallas (applause)— names which already have, from the cataract of the Green Mountains to the Missouri, from the St. John's to the misty father of waters, the Mississippi, been echoed by a free people; and there is not one of the great States which are watered by the Mississippi that is not a Democratic State. (Applause.) Some people told me when I began, to tread lightly on the Texas question. Tread lightly! Why I jumped right into it. (Applause.) I bolted straight at it, and your charms reached my heart. Ah, one maxim I have learned from the great Jackson, and that is, "A nation must obey its geography more than its constitution." The one is made by man; but those grand features which constitute geographical boundaries are written by the fingers of Him who made the world. (Loud applause.) Go on, great and mighty people; do not be daunted by one of those who say we have enough land—from your high destiny of governing in the continent—not by the shedding of blood, but by the wisdom and justice of your measures. Let those who bred it before, send in the Hessians, and we will sting them with something worse than Hessian flies. (Cheering.)

NOTES

Chapter 1. "All Rise. The Superior Court of the Territory of Orleans Is Now in Session"

1. This account is entirely factual, though I have taken a few liberties in imagining the makeup of the crowd, the courtroom scene, and the unfolding of the proceedings. It closely follows François-Xavier Martin's report of the case Territory v. Nugent, 1 Mart. (o.s.) 103 (1810), as well as Nugent's own account of the trial, which he published under the title *An Account of the Proceedings Had in the Superior Court of the Territory of Orleans, against Thierry and Nugent for Libels and Contempt of Court, with an Account of Nugent's Trial on an Indictment for a Libel* (Philadelphia, 1810). In addition to these sources, I have relied upon newspaper reports and other contemporary publications.

2. See Territory v. Thierry, 1 Mart. (o.s.) 101 (1810).

3. See "More Treason," *Orleans Gazette and Commercial Advertiser*, October 5, 1807, republished in *Trenton Federalist*, November 23, 1807.

4. As previously mentioned, one week before Nugent's trial Martin had J. B. S. Thierry imprisoned for publishing an article that improperly influenced public opinion against the prosecution of Nugent. In 1808 Judge Joshua Lewis disbarred James Workman on the ground that the latter published a story that allegedly perverted the judge's remarks concerning the conduct of Philip Grymes. In both cases, no witnesses were allowed to testify about the truth of the statements. See Jared W. Bradley, *Interim Appointment: W. C. C. Claiborne Letter Book, 1804–1805* (Baton Rouge: Louisiana State University Press, 2002), 408–9. Judge Martin also held Michel de Armas in contempt and suspended him from the practice of law for "indecorous" remarks. See Michel De Armas' Case, 10 Mart. (o.s.) 123 (1821). It was not until 1823 that the legislature restricted the contempt power to "what shall be said, done or committed directly in the presence or hearing of the court during the sitting of the same" (Meinrad Greiner, *The Louisiana Digest [1804–1841]* [New Orleans: Benjamin Levy, 1841], sec. 101, p. 21).

5. Quoted from Nugent's *Letter from His Sapient Majesty Our Sovereign Lord King Solomon, Chancellor of the Lost Will and Testament of the God Who "Bequeathed" to Us the Ocean* (New Orleans, 1809), 102. Of course, we should not trust Nugent's opinion about the quality of the translation, because he was evidently trying to disparage Martin as much as possible. Professor Olivier Moréteau, a renowned comparativist and expert on translations, has praised the quality of Martin's translation of Pothier, saying it is unmatched by the Evans

translation of 1806. See Olivier Moréteau, "François-Xavier Martin Revisited," *Louisiana Bar Journal* 60, no. 6 (2013): 475–76. Martin also translated and published several French novels, including three by Marie-Jeanne de Riccoboni. He translated her novel *Lord Rivers* in 1802. See H. G. Jones, "Martin, François-Xavier," in *Dictionary of North Carolina Biography*, ed. William S. Powell, vol. 4, L–O (Chapel Hill: University of North Carolina Press, 1991), 224–25.

6. See Nugent, *An Account of the Proceedings*, 122: "From the false report of the case of Mr. Livingston [*Livingston v. D'Orgenoy*], I have just reason to look on the whole volume as a lying catch-penny."

7. In denying the motion to recuse himself, Martin's reasoning was interesting but strange. He acknowledged that he might be recused as of right in a civil trial but not in a criminal matter. He claimed that he actually wished to recuse himself but that doing so would cause a denial of justice to the territory! See H. P. Nugent, *Defence of A. Davezac de Castras, Esq., Counsellor at Law, Now Absent, Against the Calumnies of F. X. Martin, One of the Judges of the Superior Court of the Territory of Orleans* (New Orleans, 1811), 11.

8. *Nugent*, 1 Mart. (o.s.) at 169.

9. In the announcement of Livingston's marriage to Marie-Louise-Magdaleine-Valentine Davezac Castra Moreau, the *Albany Centinel* observed that "the lady's name is rather *short*, but she is said to be majestic in person and elegant in her manners, with a *long* purse!" (marriage announcement, *Albany Centinel*, July 23, 1805).

10. In making a defense of Nugent against the charges of libel and contempt in 1808, Lewis Kerr sought an acquittal on the basis of the constitutional freedom of the press: "La liberté de la presse est d'autant plus essentielle sous un gouvernement tel qu'on pretend qu'est celui des E.U., qu'elle est la clef qui forme l'arche politique de la constitution, le vrai niveleur de la condition humaine, le rempart sans lequel la liberté civile ne pourrait se defendre un seul jour contre la tyrannie des gens en place d'un coté, et du caprice du people de l'autre" ("Au rédacteur de l'*Echo du Commerce*," *Echo du Commerce*, September 28, 1808).

11. LaVerne Thomas III, *LeDoux: A Pioneer Franco-American Family* (New Orleans: Polyanthos, 1982), 492.

12. The incident caused Nugent to sue the sheriff for damages: Nugent v. Cenas, docket number 2557, Superior Court, filed June 9, 1810. Nugent's attorney in the suit was again Auguste Davezac.

13. The text of the pamphlet was set forth in Attorney General Grymes's affidavit of May 25, 1810, which Nugent republished in *An Account of the Proceedings*.

14. The full name of the Bayou Bridge case was Orleans Navigation Co. v. Mayor, Aldermen & Inhabitants of New Orleans, 1 Mart. (o.s.) 23, 269 (1811), 2 Mart. (o.s.) 10, 214 (1812). Nugent, *An Account of the Proceedings*, 4.

15. Nugent, *An Account of the Proceedings*, 30.

16. Dormenon's Case, 1 Mart. (o.s.) 129, 132 (1810). Nugent also published an account of Dormenon's trial in *A Letter to His Excellency William C. C. Claiborne, Governor of the Territory of Orleans* (New Orleans, 1808), 106.

17. The story of the alleged debauch at the tavern was first reported in the *Orleans Gazette* and was based on information supplied by an anonymous eyewitness. Nugent's pamphlet, however, revealed the name of the anonymous witness by identifying him as none other than his own attorney, Auguste Davezac. Nugent, *An Account of the Proceedings*, 22.

18. "I am credibly informed of the truth of what appeared in the Orleans Gazette (not from me) that on the circuit, Joshua Lewis, while celebrating what he called his orgies, declared that all the charges against Mr. Dormenon had been proved. I am ready to prove both this declaration, and the bacchanalian rout by which judge Lewis and his comrades in debauch kept the tavern in a roar all night, when next day a man was to be tried for his life. I can prove that on the acquittal of this man, Judge Lewis, still reeking from the fumes of his orgies, reprimanded the sheriff for having summoned such a jury." (Nugent, *An Account of the Proceedings*, 26.)

19. The defense wished to put on four witnesses. Two of the proposed witnesses were cocounsel Holmes and Davezac, and a third was Jean Blanque. See Nugent, *A Letter to His Excellency*, 109.

20. According to William Blackstone, "It is immaterial with respect to the essence of a libel, whether the matter of it be true or false; since the provocation, and not the falsity, is the thing to be punished criminally.... In a civil action, we may remember, a libel must appear to be false, as well as scandalous; for, if the charge be true the plaintiff has received no private injury" (*Commentaries on the Laws of England* [Chicago: University of Chicago Press, 1979], 4:150). See also Marc Franklin, "The Origins and Constitutionality of Limitations on Truth as a Defense in Tort Law," *Stanford Law Review* 16, no. 4 (1964): 791.

21. "Although I regret to suffer this opportunity of making a necessary example to pass by" (*Nugent*, 1 Mart. [o.s.] at 169, 174).

22. The timing of these arrests is difficult to establish, since they were gleaned with difficulty from the pamphlet *H. P. Nugent's Reply to the Calumnies of the Honorable F. X. Martin, One of the Judges of the Superior Court of the Territory of Orleans* (Natchez, [Miss.], 1811), 17–20.

23. Ibid.

24. For example, neither Nugent nor Davezac received mention in Martin's *History of Louisiana: From the Earliest Period*, 2 vols. (New Orleans: Lyman and Beardslee, 1827); or in Charles Gayarré, *History of Louisiana*, vol. 4, *The American Domination* (New Orleans: Gresham Publishing Co., 1879).

25. See "Message," *Orleans Gazette*, April 2, 1808; "Letter of October 7th,

1808," in *Territorial Papers of the United States*, ed. Clarence Carter (Washington, D.C.: United States Government Printing Office, 1940), 9:802; George Dargo, *Jefferson's Louisiana: Politics and the Clash of Legal Traditions*, rev. ed. (1975; Clark, N.J.: Lawbook Exchange, 2009), 272.

26. The members appointed in 1806 were Villars, Boré, Watkins, Arnaud, Bouligny, and Mahon, but all of these individuals appear to have been members of the House. No appointments from the council appear to have been made. [Untitled], *Le Moniteur*, June 7, 1806. See also "Proceedings of the House," *Orleans Gazette*, February 5, 1807. In 1808 the four House members changed to Villars, Hughes, Kerr, and Lacroix. "Législature d'Orleans," *Le Moniteur*, January 27, 1808. "Lacroix" was L. Dussau de Lacroix (sometimes spelled La Croix), whom Alexander Walker identifies as "a Frenchman of the ancient régime, an exile who found in Louisiana the only sovereignty and the only soil worth fighting for" (*The Life of Andrew Jackson* [New York: Derby & Jackson, 1859], 51). "Villars" was Joseph Dubreuil de Villars, a planter described by Dargo as a man with strong Creole views and political sophistication (*Jefferson's Louisiana*, 179). "Boré" was Étienne de Boré, the famous sugar planter and first mayor of New Orleans. "Hughes" was John Hughes, a representative from Ouachita Parish who was born in county Mayo, Ireland, and was one of the first justices of the peace in Ouachita Parish. Note that the "Kerr" referred to in the text was the somewhat obscure Samuel Kerr, who represented a district outside of New Orleans, and not the better-known Lewis Kerr, who defended Nugent in his first contempt trial and authored *An Exposition of the Criminal Laws of the Territory* (New Orleans: Bradford & Anderson, 1806).

Chapter 2. The Hunt for the Lost Translators of 1808

1. A curious fact about Louisiana's first codification is its name or, to be more accurate, its *shifting* name. At no time during its planning and preparation was it ever called a digest. The project that the jurisconsults prepared over an eighteen-month period was referred to, in all preenactment legislation and newspaper reports, as the "civil code." The decision to call it the Digest of Orleans came at the eleventh hour, on the eve of enactment. Even then, the word appeared only on the title page and running heads—not once in the body of the text. Actually, the text contradicted the title page by referring on multiple occasions to the "code." There are no fewer than six references to the "present code" in both French and English in the body of the work itself. Apparently, the word "digest" on the title page (there was no title page in French) was added so hastily that these references to the "civil code" in the articles themselves were not altered or suppressed. Of course, the interior references to the "code" were written

by the jurisconsults and then translated into English. It thus appears reasonable to infer that the jurisconsults were originally instructed to produce a civil code, worked for nearly two years on that assumption, and were surprised when it was officially designated a "digest." See Vernon Valentine Palmer, "The Quest to Implant Civilian Method in Louisiana: Tracing the Origins of Judicial Methodology (the Tucker Lecture)," *Louisiana Law Review* 73, no. 3 (2013): 793. For an in-depth exploration of the mysterious meaning of the title, see Asya Ostroukh, "The Mystery of the *Mixité* around the Title of the Louisiana Digest of the Civil Laws of 1808," *Loyola Law Review* 62 (2016): 725.

2. Acts of the Legislature 1807, Territory of Orleans, April 14, 1807, chap. 21, pp. 191–92.

3. The redactors were appointed on June 7, 1806. See [Untitled], *Orleans Gazette*, July 19, 1806. Poydras's statement came in his reply to the governor of January 1807. See Dargo, *Jefferson's Louisiana*, 268.

4. Bernard Lafon, *Annuaire louisianais pour l'année 1809* (New Orleans: Lafon, 1808), 164.

5. The irony is that earlier the same day the "civil code" was enacted as a "digest"; now it reverted again to a "civil code"!

6. Acts of the Legislature 1808, Territory of Orleans, March 31, 1808, chap. 29, p. 92, emphasis added.

7. William C. C. Claiborne to Thomas Jefferson, January 15, 1808, Founders Online, National Archives, http://founders.archives.gov/documents/Jefferson/99-01-02-7205.

8. Vincent Nolte, *Fifty Years in Both Hemispheres; or, Reminiscences of a Merchant's Life* (London: Redfield, 1854), 109.

9. Records show that Davezac was disbarred by Judge Joshua Lewis in December 1808 but almost immediately reinstated. See Bradley, *Interim Appointment*, 408–9. His disbarment was changed to a reprimand.

10. See the announcement of the partnership in the *Orleans Gazette and Commercial Advertiser*, April 28, 1818, 2.

11. Reported in the *Otsego Herald* (Cooperstown, N.Y.), June 15, 1815, 1. Like Nugent, Davezac was prepared to go beyond forensic translation. Davezac circulated an advertisement in which he sought subscribers for his proposed translation of Ville-Hardouin's *Conquête de Constantinople*. See "Proposed Works," advertisement, *North American Review* 24 (1827): 263.

12. See, for example, Nugent, *Defence of A. Davezac de Castras*, 42: "I placed myself next to Mr. Le Clerc, to interpret for him." See also Nugent, *An Account of the Proceedings*, 6.

13. See "Enclosure: Thomas Jefferson's List of Batture-Related Papers and Pamphlets Sent to Counsel, 23 March 1811," Founders Online, National Archives,

https://founders.archives.gov/documents/Jefferson/03-03-02-0368-0002. Nugent's commission to translate a letter from Daniel Clark to the mayor of New Orleans is mentioned in the pages of the *Louisiana Courier*, dated March 1811.

14. See also Jean-Bon Saint-André, *A Summary Journal of the Cruise Undertaken for the Purpose of Protecting the Chesapeake Convoy, by the Fleet of the French Republic* (Philadelphia: Benjamin Franklin Bache, 1794). See [Untitled], *Aurora General Advertiser* (Philadelphia), July 14, 1795, 1.

15. Erica Robin Johnson, "Louisiana Identity on Trial: The Superior Court Case of Pierre Benonime Dormenon" (master's thesis, University of Texas at Arlington, 2007), https://rc.library.uta.edu/uta-ir/bitstream/handle/10106/622/umi-uta-1842.pdf?sequence=1&isAllowed=y. This gesture cemented a friendship for life between the two men. For Nugent's account of the trial, see H. P. Nugent, *Observations on the Trial of Peter Dormenon, Esquire* (New Orleans: Printed for the author, 1809).

16. In today's money, $250 corresponds to approximately $4,790 and was not a minor governmental expenditure. It must be remembered that it was only a part payment. See www.measuringworth.com. This sum reflects the purchasing power of $250 in present dollars, using the consumer price index as the measure. If one wished to measure the "economic status" of $250 or, put another way, its relative "prestige value" today, it would amount to $127,000, as measured by nominal GDP per capita. Thus by either measure the sum was not a minor expenditure.

17. For example, "Mr. Missonet" was Pierre-François Missonet. He served as the city recorder from 1804 on and was perhaps still serving as such in 1808. Governor Claiborne appointed him justice of the peace in 1809. See William C. C. Claiborne, *Official Letter Books of W. C. C. Claiborne, 1801–1816*, ed. Dunbar Rowland (Jackson, Miss.: State Department of History and Archives, 1917), 4:385. "Mr. Cuvillier" was Pierre-Amboise Cuvillier, who served in 1809 as deputy register of the Court of Proofs of the Territory of Orleans. See Rosemonde and Emile Kuntz Collection, 1804–50, folder 41, Special Collections, Tulane University, New Orleans. Later on in his career, Cuvillier served as clerk to the state Senate. "Mr. Vassant" can be identified as the first clerk in the Secretary's Office of the City of New Orleans. "Mr. Dupin," who received $125, was probably Simon Dupin, but this is not certain. Two remaining names, Gourdet ($70) and Pomet ($10), could not be identified.

18. The sums received by Nugent and Davezac were commensurate with the payment the translators could have expected, but an inconvenient discrepancy should be mentioned. Under the payment scheme outlined in the statute of April 14, 1807, the translators were to receive two-fifths of $750 upon the completion of their work. By that calculation the final payment would have been $300 apiece, whereas Nugent and Davezac only received $250, which is an ap-

parent $50 underpayment. The underpayment is at variance with the thesis that they were in fact the translators of the digest. Perhaps there is elsewhere some documentation explaining away the discrepancy, but research has not been able to unearth it. On the present evidence it can only be said that the payment comes rather close to the anticipated sum, and the discrepancy may be eventually resolved by more research. This discrepancy might be cleared up if we had in hand the disbursements by the territorial treasurer, George W. Morgan, but the treasury warrants of the territory are not available. According to a resolution of the territorial legislature, the legislative committee charged with the revision of the code was empowered to make appropriations for "the expences incurred by the copies, translations, and the like" and "to issue warrants for that purpose on the treasurer of this territory." See [Untitled], *Orleans Gazette and Commercial Advertiser*, July 19, 1806. By an Act of the Legislature, Territory of Orleans, March 31, 1808, chap. 29, pp. 95ff., governing the records kept by the treasurer of the territory, all warrants must state the date, name, nature of the claim, and legal authorization.

19. Significantly, Auguste's grandson was baptized Edward Livingston Davezac.

20. Livingston's relationship with Moreau-Lislet, however, was not always perfectly cordial. On one occasion in 1808, Judge Moreau-Lislet reportedly insulted Livingston in open court, and Livingston challenged him to a duel. Moreau-Lislet, however, apologized, and the matter was dropped. See "Extract of a Letter from New Orleans, November 29, 1808," *Connecticut Herald*, January 24, 1809. What a calamity it would have been if Louisiana's two greatest lawgivers had assassinated themselves in a senseless duel!

21. See chapter 4.

22. Brown received a share of the batture property as compensation for his legal services. See Preston, Executor of James Brown v. Richard Keene, 39 U.S. 133 (1840). On Brown's preference for Livingston, see Bradley, *Interim Appointment*, 262–63.

23. Quoted in Dargo, *Jefferson's Louisiana*, 203. See also John T. Hood Jr., "History and Development of the Louisiana Civil Code," *Louisiana Law Review* 19, no. 1 (1958): 18.

24. W. C. C. Claiborne to James Madison, September 7, 1808, in Claiborne, *Official Letter Books*.

25. See Bernard Lafon, *Calendrier de commerce de la Nouvelle-Orléans* (New Orleans: Lafon, 1807), 72–73.

26. See Dan Degges, "The Mexican Association: The Secret Society behind the Aaron Burr Conspiracy" (unpublished manuscript, University of Arkansas at Monticello), www.academia.edu/4358596/The_Mexican_Association.

27. W. C. C. Claiborne to James Madison: "Workman and Kerr, were en-

gaged in Burr's conspiracy, and have since been expel'ed my presence; Daversac [*sic*] was strongly suspected, and to say the least of him is a most unprincipled frenchman."

28. See Baptism, Diocese of New Orleans Sacramental Records, February 3, 1817, New Orleans.

29. See Nugent v. Roland, 12 Mart. (o.s.) 659 (La. 1821).

30. See Nugent, *A Letter to His Excellency*, 1–12, 8.

Chapter 3. Henry Paul Nugent: The Story of a Mercurial Man

1. His parents' names are stated in full in his 1812 marriage certificate. His date of birth can be found on a site in Ancestry.com, http://person.ancestry.com/tree/79793211/person/32411047160/facts.

2. H. P. Nugent, *A Philippic against the Calumniator of the Immortal Washington* (Charleston: Thomas Bowen, 1801), 25.

3. [Untitled], *Daily Picayune*, August 22, 1896.

4. "The Art of Reading" probably refers to the academy in Bath founded in 1770 by Thomas Sheridan (1718–88) for "young gentlemen in the art of reading and reciting and grammatical knowledge of the English tongue" (J. T. Scharf and Thompson Westcott, *History of Philadelphia, 1609–1884* [Philadelphia, 1884], 2:962).

5. The third edition (1790) was printed in London by G. Bourne and T. Turner. A reprinted third edition (1791) was printed by J. Sullivan in Cork.

6. See H. P. Nugent, *Mr. Nugent's Vindication of His Writings, in a Letter to Mr. Lilly* (Albany, 1799), 17; Nugent, *Observations on the Trial*, 30: "I was, in that year [1793], translator to Mr. Genêt in New-York and Philadelphia"; [Untitled], *Albany Gazette*, November 30, 1798. Nugent's claim that his meeting with Genêt was rather accidental is at odds with Eberhard Faber's statement that Nugent arrived in America in 1793 as Genêt's interpreter. See Eberhard Faber, *Building the Land of Dreams: New Orleans and the Transformation of Early America* (Princeton, N.J.: Princeton University Press, 2016), 130.

7. Talleyrand spent the years 1794–96 in Philadelphia. John L. Earl III, "Talleyrand in Philadelphia," *Pennsylvania Magazine of History and Biography* 91 (1967): 282–98.

8. Nugent, *Mr. Nugent's Vindication*, 13. Nugent wrote in 1808 that "Mr. Talleyrand, now prince of Benevento, and all the illustrious Frenchmen then in Philadelphia, treated me with great friendship" (*A Letter to His Excellency*, 12). In Philadelphia, newspapers record that Nugent became involved in a petty dispute with a tavern owner whose waiters, according to Nugent, filled wine glasses before receiving orders from customers. The tavern owner responded indig-

nantly. [Untitled], *Philadelphia General Advertiser*, August 29, 1794, September 4, 1794.

9. The Philadelphia newspapers noted that he performed in the comic opera *The Maid of the Mill* and in *The Sailor's Landlady* in 1794 and 1795. [Untitled], *Philadelphia Gazette and Universal Daily Advertiser*, January 18, 1794, 3; [Untitled], *Gazette of the United States*, January 6, 1795, 2.

10. See [Untitled], *Massachusetts Mercury*, January 8, 1796, 2. See also [Untitled], *Albany Gazette*, November 16, 1798, 2.

11. [Untitled], *Albany Gazette*, November 30, 1798.

12. Nugent, *Mr. Nugent's Vindication*, 18. Nugent penned a poem entitled "The Challenge," which began: "I sing of a prig who, inept as a fool, / Contends that all Yankees should still go to school, / For to him ev'ry yankee's so silly a dupe, / That of reason he knows not the prow from the poop."

13. See ibid., 26.

14. See [Untitled], *Maryland Gazette*, December 19, 1799, where he proposed to open a school at the Ballroom on December 13, 1799.

15. See "To the Ladies and Gentlemen, Natives of Ireland, Settled in this City," *City Gazette* (Charleston), May 20, 1801.

16. The Charleston ad appeared in the *Independent Gazetteer*, February 15, 1805, 1. The Natchez advertisement was substantially similar. *Mississippi Herald and Natchez Gazette*, December 23, 1806.

17. Richard W. Bailey, "The Foundation of English in the Louisiana Purchase: New Orleans, 1800–1850," *American Speech* 78 (2003): 363–84.

18. Quoted in George Dargo, *Colony to Empire: Episodes in American Legal History* (Clark, N.J.: Lawbook Exchange, 2011), 183.

19. Thomas Klinger points out that Colonial French differed little from Standard French in syntax and morphology, though, depending on the speaker, it may diverge from Standard French phonologically and lexically. Thomas A. Klinger, "Language Labels and Language Use among Cajuns and Creoles in Louisiana," University of Pennsylvania Working Papers in Linguistics, vol. 9, no. 2, 2003, 79, https://repository.upenn.edu/cgi/viewcontent.cgi?article=1454&context=pwpl.

20. See Gabriel Debien and René LeGardeur, "Les colons de Saint-Domingue réfugiés á la Louisiane (1792–1804)," *Revue de la Louisiane* 10, no. 2 (Winter 1981): 132; Paul Lachance, "The Foreign French," in *Creole New Orleans*, ed. Arnold R. Hirsch and Joseph Logsdon (Baton Rouge: Louisiana State University Press, 1992), 105; Vernon Valentine Palmer, "Setting the Scene: Louisiana 1803–1812," in *The Louisiana Civilian Experience: Critiques of Codification in a Mixed Jurisdiction* (Durham, N.C.: Carolina Academic Press, 2005), 5.

21. See Aimee Jeanne Carlisle, "Language Attrition in Louisiana Creole French" (honors thesis, University of California, Davis, 2010), https://www

.yumpu.com/en/document/view/38092426/language-attrition-in-louisiana-creole-french. Carlisle describes how Plantation Society French, which was positioned at the top of the linguistic hierarchy in the eighteenth century, was demoted to second place during the period 1803–12 and replaced by English. As a result, the hierarchy ranged from high to low in this order: Standard American English, then Plantation Society French (the closest variant to Standard French, spoken in France), then Cajun French (the Acadian French of immigrants from France's Canadian territories), and finally Louisiana Creole French (the most stigmatized of French dialects, spoken by the ethnically Creole population of African descent). Ibid., 44.

22. Marietta Marie Lebreton, "A History of the Territory of Orleans, 1803–1812" (PhD diss., Louisiana State University, 1969), 290ff., LSU Historical Dissertations and Theses 1554.

23. Quoted from Nugent, *Letter from His Sapient Majesty*, 102. For a history of the public school system, see Raleigh A. Suarez, "Chronicle of a Failure: Public Education in Antebellum Louisiana," *Louisiana History: The Journal of the Louisiana Historical Association* 12, no. 2 (Spring 1971): 109–22; Martin L. Riley, "The Development of Education in Louisiana prior to Statehood," *Louisiana Historical Quarterly* 19 (July 1936): 622–24; Stuart Grayson Noble, "Governor Claiborne and the Public School System of the Territorial Government of Louisiana," *Louisiana Historical Quarterly* 11, no. 4 (October 1928): 538.

24. Faber, *Building the Land of Dreams*, 123.

25. On the "unexpected collapse" of the French language in Louisiana, see Palmer, *The Louisiana Civilian Experience*, 16–18.

26. Vernon Valentine Palmer, ed., *Mixed Jurisdictions Worldwide: The Third Legal Family*, 2nd ed. (Cambridge: Cambridge University Press, 2012), 279.

27. Ibid.

28. Quoted in Nathalie Dessens, "The Sounds of Babel: Staging American Ethnic Diversity in Early Nineteenth-Century New Orleans," special issue, *Complutense Journal of English Studies* 23 (2015): 24.

29. Thus, under the Practice Act of 1805, the petitions and answers exchanged in civil causes before the Superior Court had to be written in both English and French. See Acts of the Legislature, Territory of Orleans, April 10, 1805, chap. 26, secs. 2 and 5. Moreover, the 1808 Digest of Orleans was promulgated in a bilingual edition in which the English and French versions were regarded as coequal in authority.

30. Quoted in Gayarré, *History of Louisiana*, 4:201.

31. Nugent, *An Account of the Proceedings*, 39. Their names were John Gourjon Jun., William Montgomery, René Delarue, Thomas Elmes, Rouques Jun., Judah Touro, Frederick Giraud, Jean Lanusse, Joseph Fry, F. Aimé, G. Dubuys, and William Lester.

32. For a summary account of the legislation, see Vernon Valentine Palmer, "Sounding the Retreat: The Exit of Spanish Law in Early Louisiana," *Tulane European & Civil Law Forum* 31/32 (2017): 121–56.

33. See Vernon Valentine Palmer, "The Strange Science of Codifying Slavery: Moreau Lislet and the Louisiana Digest of 1808," *Tulane European & Civil Law Forum* 24 (2009): 83–113.

34. The obituary of Alexander Dimitry (1805–83), who was one of Nugent's students, stated that Nugent was an Irish patriot who opened a school attended by the children of the most respectable citizens of the city, including the Lewises, the Hunters, the Conrads, the Kenners, the Cenases, and the Stewarts. See [Untitled], *Times Picayune*, January 30, 1883. According to Stuart Noble, in 1811 he may have operated this school jointly with McKinsey. Stuart Grayson Noble, "Schools of New Orleans during the First Quarter of the Nineteenth Century," *Louisiana Historical Quarterly* 14, no. 1 (January 1931): 65, 68.

35. [Untitled], *L'Ami des lois et journal du soir*, December 2, 1816. In this article, Nugent wrote, "With the assistance of Mrs. Nugent, he teaches children of both sexes, from their first going to school. In the evening he teaches English, French and Spanish, to grown gentlemen."

36. *Le Télégraphe et le Commercial Advertiser* was published in New Orleans between 1803 and 1812.

37. Though this identification is not free from doubt, it appears that the speaker in question was Colonel Bellechasse and that he was referring to "the possession of the Batture by the proprietor." See "Extract of a Letter from a Gentleman in New Orleans, dated September 17, 1807," *Political Observatory* (Walpole, N.H.), September 17, 1807. On the same day, Colonel Macarty addressed the audience about the batture question and criticized the decision of the court, which ruled in Livingston's favor, so it may have been this speech that Nugent translated. See the account of Gayarré, *History of Louisiana*, 4:185–89.

38. "I'm Davus not Oedipus" (Terence, *Andria* 1.2). Nugent was in effect saying, I am just a simple man: I cannot solve riddles like Oedipus.

39. The Latin phrase may be translated as "For words ought to be understood in such a way that they may have some effect, so that the instrument may rather be valid than void."

40. [Untitled], *Orleans Gazette and Commercial Advertiser*, August 31, 1807.

41. "More Treason!," *Orleans Gazette and Commercial Advertiser*.

42. [Untitled], *Le Télégraphe et le Commercial Advertiser*, October 13, 1807. Nugent suggested that the court's judgment in favor of Livingston was the product of judicial bias, "a false judgment of judges Mathews and Lewis, judge Sprigg dissenting, without a jury, the judges being the intimate companions and convivial guests of Mr. Livingston, who was known to be jointly interested in the suit with his client."

43. See Superior Court docket, 1809–13, numbers 2950–54, 2557, and city court docket numbers 2401, 2578, and 2579, held in the New Orleans Public Library. The majority of these were to enforce promissory notes drawn in Nugent's favor. See, for example, Nugent v. Delhomme, 2 Mart. (o.s.) 307 (1812); Nugent v. Trepagnier, 2 Mart. (o.s.) 205 (1812).

44. See notes 85–87 below.

45. The anecdote appears in Nugent, *Observations on the Trial*, 28.

46. The first arrest was on December 24, 1807, the second was on May 25, 1810 (see the case of Territory v. Nugent, 1 Mart. [o.s.] 91 [1810]), and the third was in January 1811.

47. Nugent recounted the episode in *A Letter to His Excellency*.

48. Cenas's insult to Nugent was "You are below my notice, I knew you in Philadelphia," thus insinuating that Nugent's character in Philadelphia was infamous.

49. The news account originated in New Orleans and was dated February 2, 1808. The site of publication has not been found. It was republished in New York in the [Untitled], *Oracle and Daily Advertiser*, March 25, 1808.

50. In *A Letter to His Excellency*, however, Nugent reproached the governor for delaying the pardon and for not ordering his immediate release from prison.

51. Johnson, "Louisiana Identity," 66.

52. [Untitled], *Le Moniteur de la Louisiane*, May 4, 1808, 1, my translation. Other examples of his writings are collected in the appendix to the present volume.

53. See Nugent, *A Philippic*, 54–55.

54. Nugent, *An Account of the Proceedings*, 67, 102.

55. Nugent, *Defence of A. Davezac de Castras*, 10.

56. Ibid., 4.

57. Ibid. He returned to the subject of his critical review in another diatribe: Nugent, *An Account of the Proceedings*, 66.

58. Nugent, *Defence of A. Davezac de Castras*, 7.

59. Ibid., 11.

60. Martin was a notable eccentric. H. G. Jones writes: "Always a frugal man, he became more eccentric with age, grasping every dollar in sight and spending as little as a miser. He was even accused of refusing to pay the twenty-dollar cost of burying his body servant, who died on one of his circuit travels; he denied the obligation to pay the debt inasmuch as he did not live in the district of the burial, but he did offer one dollar, which he considered generous for the burial of a black servant. Martin, whose eyesight was never good, became increasingly blind in the 1830s, and with the affliction, he was a pitiful figure. He lived in squalid quarters and dressed little better than a beggar. As he felt his way along

the streets of New Orleans, his eyes closed, he was often taunted by mischievous children" ("Martin, François-Xavier," 224–25).

61. Michael Chiorazzi, "François-Xavier Martin: Printer, Lawyer, Jurist," *Duke Law Magazine* 7, no. 1 (Winter 1989): 16. Historians have generally portrayed Martin as avaricious and frugal. "His passion for riches," writes Warren Billings, "was no less than his devotion to law. . . . A lifelong bachelor, Martin was economical to the point of being abstemious" ("A Judicial Legacy: The Last Will and Testament of Francois-Xavier Martin," *Louisiana History: The Journal of the Louisiana Historical Association* 25 [1984]: 278). Michael Chiorazzi sees him as a "solitary miser whose only love was the law" ("Francois-Xavier Martin," 11).

62. Nugent, *Defence of A. Davezac de Castras*, 40.

63. Ibid., 15.

64. See "Liberalism in New Orleans," *Quarto*, no. 113 (June 1976).

65. Anna Beck, a native of Belfast, Ireland, was Antoine's third wife (according to information in Thomas, *LeDoux*, 494). His first marriage in 1742 was to Elisabeth LeSeigneur, and his second was to Marie Margueritte Dumoulin in 1782.

66. See Blanche Maurel, "Une Société de pensée à Saint-Domingue, le 'Cercle des Philadelphes' au Cap Français," *Revue française d'histoire d'outre-mer* 48 (1961): 234–66.

67. See the index of names, Moreau de St. Méry, under "Ruotte," http://www.ghcaraibe.org/livres/ouvdiv/stmery-R.html. The record of Nugent and Ruotte's marriage at St. Louis Cathedral noted that the bride's father was "the dean" of the Superior Council. No doubt this title was a point of family pride. Cathedral records also show the marriage of Josephine's sister Marguerite on April 24, 1807, to Jean-Baptiste Giboin Tomatis, with her mother, Anna, as witness.

68. According to LaVerne Thomas III (*LeDoux*, 494), he died in Charleston in 1796.

69. See the acts of sale passed before Pedesclaux on September 4, 1805, in which Anna Beck, Veuve Ruotte, sold two slaves, Jone and Betsey, aged thirty and eighteen years, respectively, to Labatut for a price of 1,640 piastres. Louisiana Slave Records, documents 253, 254, ibiblio.org/laslave/individ.php?sid =39542. In light of the French proclamations abolishing slavery on the island, the two slaves may have been "re-enslaved" by the Ruottes when they were brought to New Orleans. See Rebecca Scott, "Paper Thin: Freedom and Re-enslavement in the Diaspora of the Haitian Revolution," *Law and History Review* 29 (2011): 1061.

70. Faber, *Building the Land of Dreams*, 138–39 (noting a long list of such matches).

71. [Untitled], *L'Ami des lois et journal du soir*, December 2, 1816.

114 NOTES TO CHAPTER THREE

72. [Untitled], *L'Ami des lois et journal du soir*, November 3, 1814; Thomas, *LeDoux*, 492.

73. [Untitled], *Albany Gazette*, April 23, 1815. The Lancaster method of education was named after Joseph Lancaster (1778–1838), who led a nineteenth-century movement to establish schools in which more advanced students taught less advanced ones, enabling a small number of schoolmasters to teach large numbers of students at low cost.

74. [Untitled], *L'Ami des lois et journal du soir*, December 2, 1816. I am grateful to James Karst for calling this reference to my attention.

75. Robert Vogel, "*Historical Memoir of the War in West Florida and Louisiana in 1814–1815, with an Atlas*," book review, *Louisiana History* 42, no. 1 (Winter 2001): 113–15.

76. Nugent v. Chancellor & Regents of the College of Orleans, docket number 438, Eastern District, July 1823, document A.

77. Noble, "Schools of New Orleans," 74.

78. See H. P. Nugent v. Chancellor & Regents of the College of Orleans, docket number 438, Eastern District, July 1823, document A, p. 181.

79. "Gulliver's Account," *Louisiana Gazette*, November 16, 1819, an extract of which is found in document D, Nugent v. Chancellor.

80. Nugent v. Chancellor.

81. The appeal was pending in the state supreme court when Nugent died in 1822, which made the issue of his reinstatement moot. See H. P. Nugent, docket number 438, Eastern District, July 1823.

82. The 1820 census records the family as living at "Islands of the Falls River" (a mutilation of False River or Fausse Rivière).

83. Thomas, *LeDoux*, 214, 493.

84. Transcript at 11, Nugent v. Roland (La. 1823). According to LaVerne Thomas, the home provided to Nugent was on the property of planter Charles Stewart. Thomas, *LeDoux*, 493.

85. The document filed with the Senate refers to Judge "Henault," apparently one of many imaginative attempts to spell this jurist's name. In some accounts, his name is spelled "Esnaud" or "Einault." Louis Esneault was a trial judge in Pointe Coupée who presided over the case of Nugent v. Roland, 12 Mart. (o.s.) 659 (La. 1823). Nugent's complaint to the Senate, however, apparently concerned the judge's conduct in some earlier case or perhaps his conduct off the bench. It is incredible to note that in 1822 Judge Esneault fought a duel—a sword fight *with sabres*—and killed fellow judge Philogene Favrot, of Baton Rouge. Judge Esneault was gravely wounded. [Untitled], *Courrier de la Louisiane*, February 20, 1822.

86. *Journal of the Senate*, January 9, 1822.

87. See Nugent v. Roland, 12 Mart (o.s.) 659 (La. 1823).

88. Under an 1821 act of the legislature, the organization of the parish schools changed. The supervisory power previously held by the police juries was transferred to five trustees appointed by the police juries, and the trustees would determine the qualifications of teachers and control the apportionment of money contributed by the state. See Suarez, "Chronicle of a Failure," 113.

89. See H. P. Nugent v. Louis Chenevert (4th District 1822); H. P. Nugent v. Auguste Provosty (4th District 1822); H. P. Nugent v. B. Louis L'Hermite (4th District 1822).

90. Obituary, Diocese of Baton Rouge Catholic Church Records (vol. 4, 1820–29; repr., 2014), 436.

91. Transcript, *Nugent v. Roland*, 9. LaVerne Thomas has speculated that Nugent may have been killed in a duel with Dr. Auguste Provosty, the president of the Pointe Coupée School Board, but I have not been able to substantiate that theory.

92. Thomas, *LeDoux*, 493.

93. His admission to the bar is dated May 8, 1822. Supreme Court Rolls 2:221.

94. He represented himself "in propria personam" in the above-noted cases, filed in 1822.

Chapter 4. Auguste Davezac de Castera: The Life of an Eloquent *Docteur*

1. Janice Deitch Young, *The Barrosse and Davezac Families* (Metairie, La.: Private publication, 2002), 417.

2. Born in 1768, Margaret died on September 5, 1847, in Accomac, Virginia, at seventy-nine years of age.

3. Davezac's son, Auguste Jr., was a doctor and practiced in New Orleans. His practice is mentioned in newspaper reports in the 1840s and 1850s. See [Untitled], *Times-Picayune*, October 7, 1853. Auguste Jr. married Sarah Carter of Kentucky, and in 1840 they had a son, whom they piously named Edward Livingston Davezac. One account states that Auguste was present in New Orleans when Louisiana was transferred to the United States; however, this appears to be an error. See the biographical account of his life: "Major Davezac," *United States Magazine and Democratic Review* 16 (1845): 109–10.

4. Janice Deitch Young points out that "this was only a remnant of the large, three generation d'Avezac de Castera family from St. Domingue. Much later, the family learned that an aunt had escaped to France and it would be many years before an uncle would be reunited with them" (*The Barrosse and Davezac Families*, 418).

5. A notice in *Le Moniteur* of June 10, 1807, stated that "Le Docteur Auguste Davezac a établi son domicile dans la maison de M. Méricalt, rue Royale Sud."

See also the mention that "Dr. Davezac" was elected a director of the Bibliothèque de Société. [Untitled], *Le Moniteur*, January 30, 1808.

6. Nolte, *Fifty Years*, 89.

7. Louise Livingston Hunt, *Memoir of Mrs. Edward Livingston* (New York, 1886), 38. The Collège d'Orléans, established in 1805, was in existence for merely twenty years.

8. He received many accolades for his translation into French of Sir Walter Scott's poem "Marmion." See the review of it in "French Translation of Marmion," *Port Folio*, 3rd ser., 2, no. 1 (July 1813): 631ff.

9. See "Administrations of the Mayors of New Orleans: Louis Philippe Joseph de Roffignac (1766–1846)," Louisiana Division New Orleans Public Library, http://nutrias.org/info/louinfo/admins/roffignac.htm.

10. Charles Havens Hunt, *Life of Edward Livingston* (New York: Appleton & Co., 1864), 276.

11. Ibid.

12. Lachance, "The Foreign French," 104. Elizabeth Gaspard gives this description of legal apprenticing: "City law offices became the training ground for prospective attorneys who served their apprenticeships there. Such an education was not unusual, as apprenticeship was the prevalent method of studying law in the United States during most of the antebellum period. In fact, only a tiny minority of the pioneer lawyers were law-school graduates. An apprentice 'read law' in the office of an established attorney. That meant that he usually did the scut work around the office, such as copying briefs, running errands, collecting fees, and only occasionally doing research for cases. In this way, he was introduced to the mysteries of the profession. The quality of the education a student received naturally depended upon the competence and diligence of the attorney under whom he studied as well as the selection of books available in the attorney's law library." ("The Rise of the Louisiana Bar: The Early Period, 1813–1839," *Louisiana History* 28, no. 2 [Spring 1987]: 183, 187.)

13. The sentence was later reduced to a reprimand.

14. The conviction was overturned on grounds that the indictment was defective. Territory v. Nugent, 1 Mart. (o.s.) 103 (1810). See also Detournion v. Dormenon, 1 Mart. (o.s.) 137 (1810), in which Davezac represented a plaintiff who was charged with contempt of court. See also Territory v. Durossat et al., 2 Mart (o.s.) 120 (1812).

15. See Gaspard, "The Rise of the Louisiana Bar," 183.

16. Young, *The Barrosse and Davezac Families*, 419. See also William C. Davis, *The Pirates Laffite: The Treacherous World of the Corsairs of the Gulf* (Orlando: Harcourt, 2005), 226.

17. Nolte, *Fifty Years*, 207.

18. "Major Davezac," 110; see also the entry by Jan Onofrio, "D'Avezac, Au-

guste Geneviève Valentin," in *Louisiana Biographical Dictionary* (St. Clair Shores, Mich.: Somerset Publishers, 1999), 73. As an example of his oratorical powers, see the argument for a rehearing in Steel v. Cazeaux, 8 Mart. (o.s.) 318 (1820).

19. Onofrio, "D'Avezac, Auguste Geneviève Valentin," 73.
20. This was confirmed by a Westlaw scan of the cases.
21. See references about him in the *Acts of the Second Session of the Legislature*, 1816, chap. 30, pp. 60–61.
22. [Untitled], *Courrier de la Louisiane*, March 10, 1823, 6.
23. Ibid. Quoted in Young, *The Barrosse and Davezac Families*, 419.
24. Quoted from Pamela Keyes, "Auguste Davezac, the Creole Celebrity That History Forgot," *Historia Obscura*, October 2, 2018, https://www.historiaobscura.com/auguste-davezac-the-creole-celebrity-that-history-forgot/.
25. Henry Stuart Foote, *The Bench and Bar of the South and Southwest* (New York, 1876), 194.
26. Onofrio, "D'Avezac, Auguste Geneviève Valentin," 72–73.

Chapter 5. Reexamining and Exhuming a Pioneer Translation

1. "Letter of October 7th, 1808," 802. The governor had been less critical of the translation in his initial message to the public six months earlier. See "Message." As George Dargo characterized the governor's earlier view, "He pointed to weaknesses in the English translation but was satisfied that no inconvenience would be caused by it" (*Jefferson's Louisiana*, 272).
2. Act of the Legislature, Territory of Orleans, March 31, 1808, chap. 29, p. 120, sec. 5.
3. The evolution of the "French-preference rule" in the courts is traced by Roger K. Ward, "The French Language in Louisiana Law and Legal Education: A Requiem," *Louisiana Law Review* 57, no. 4 (Summer 1997): 1283–1324.
4. Edward B. Dubuisson, "The Codes of Louisiana (Originals Written in French; Errors of Translation)," in *Report of the Louisiana Bar Association, Vol. 25, for 1924* (New Orleans: Montgomery-Andree Printing Co., 1924), 143–55. Calling it a "hack" translation, Dubuisson appealed to the legislature for urgent revision. Edward Dubuisson, "Errors of Translation in the Codes," *Loyola Law Journal* 5, no. 3 (May 1924): 164, 174ff.
5. Dubuisson, "The Codes of Louisiana," 149.
6. Roger Ward, "The Death of the French Language in Louisiana Law," in *Louisiana: Microcosm of a Mixed Jurisdiction*, ed. Vernon V. Palmer (Durham, N.C.: Carolina Academic Press, 1999), 53; Ward, "The French Language," 1283.
7. Nearly every aspect of the digest has been questioned or contested. There has been passionate controversy about the French or Spanish provenance of the

provisions (the Pascal/Batiza debate) and disagreement over whether the document was a true code or only a digest. Various claims have been made over whether the jurisconsults violated their legislative instructions, whether natural law thinking played a role in the drafting, and whether the intriguing de la Vergne volume (a hand-annotated copy of the digest possessed and composed by Moreau-Lislet himself) represents a list of his sources (Pascal) or a set of concordances (Batiza), or if it amounts to the jurisconsult's "positive law alibi" (Baade).

8. See my remarks in "The Man behind the de la Vergne Volume," paper presented at the conference "A Celebration of the Civil Law," Tulane University Law School, November 6, 2019.

9. For similar quotes from other contemporaries, see my chapter "Understanding Moreau Lislet: The Recent Discovery of His System of Omissions," in Palmer, *The Louisiana Civilian Experience*, 25n24.

10. Quoted in George Dargo, "Louisiana's First Civil Law Digest," in Dargo, *Colony to Empire*, 163–64.

11. [Untitled], *La Lanterne magique*, February 18, 1809. George Dargo refers to this reprint as "the barbarous yoke" article.

12. Rodolfo Batiza, "Origins of Modern Codification of the Civil Law: The French Experience and Its Implications for Louisiana Law," *Tulane Law Review* 56, no. 2 (February 1982): 477, 584–85.

13. Seth Brostoff, "The Encyclopedist Code: *Ancien Droit* French Legal Encyclopedias and Their Verbatim Influence on the Louisiana Digest of 1808," *Journal of Civil Law Studies* 13 (forthcoming).

14. Robert Pascal, "Sources of the Digest of 1808: A Reply to Professor Batiza," *Tulane Law Review* 46, no. 4 (April 1972): 603.

15. Robert Pascal, "Of the Civil Code and Us," in *Robert Anthony Pascal: A Priest of Right Order*, ed. Olivier Moréteau (Baton Rouge: Claitor's, 2010), 133.

16. For example, the places originally identified in which Blackstone appears are the titles dealing with the rules of interpretation, master and servant, father and child, and communities and corporations. On common-law words of art, see the discussion below relating to "inheritance," "fruits," and "profits."

17. Dargo, *Jefferson's Louisiana*. See also Elizabeth Gaspar Brown, "Legal Systems in Conflict: Orleans Territory 1804–1812," *American Journal of Legal History* 1, no. 1 (January 1957): 35–75.

18. Palmer, *Mixed Jurisdictions Worldwide*, 71–74. See also Marc Fernandez, *From Chaos to Continuity* (Baton Rouge: Louisiana State University Press, 2001), 112–13.

19. See Wendell Holmes and Symeon Symeonides, "Representation, Mandate and Agency: A Kommentar on Louisiana's New Law," *Tulane Law Review* 73, no. 4 (March 1999): 1104.

20. Professor Dainow deemed the word "consideration" in this article as a mistranslation (see Joseph Dainow, ed., *1972 Compiled Edition of the Civil Codes of Louisiana* [St. Paul, Minn.: West Publishing Co., 1973], 17:794), yet, although the word is a red flag to a civilian, it is little different from the many examples of transposed common-law terminology that the learned editor did not treat as a mistranslation. Thus, as a matter of consistency, it is difficult to understand why he saw a mistranslation here and not in the other cases.

21. In its seventh meaning in *Webster's 3rd New International Dictionary* (2002), "cant" means an auction and has an Irish derivation.

22. Some of these terms worked their way into the alphabetical index placed at the front of the digest (these terms do not appear in the French index), thus pointing anglophone readers to the pages where they appeared.

23. Act of the Legislature, Territory of Orleans, June 3, 1806, chap. 16, p. 70.

24. Act of the Legislature, Territory of Orleans, May 21, 1806, chap. 11, p. 44.

25. Act of the Legislature, Territory of Orleans, May 26, 1806, chap. 14, p. 64.

26. Act of the Legislature, Territory of Orleans, March 20, 1809, chap. 26, p. 72.

27. Act of the Legislature, Territory of Orleans, April 10, 1805, chap. 29, p. 304.

28. Act of the Legislature, Territory of Orleans, March 31, 1808, chap. 30, p. 129.

29. Mitchell Franklin, "Some Observations on the Influence of French Law on the Early Civil Codes of Louisiana," in *Le Droit civil français: Livre-souvenir des journées du droit civil français* (Paris: Le Barreau de Montréal, 1936), 844. See also Michael McAuley, "The Pedagogical Code," *Louisiana Law Review* 63, no. 4 (Summer 2003): 1293.

30. Franklin, "Some Observations," 841.

31. Nevertheless, some pedagogic material can be found in the French-language texts of the digest. Moreau-Lislet and Brown had a pedagogic purpose when they drew upon *ancien droit* encyclopedias to provide ready-made French-language definitions of key concepts and to supply supplementary rules explaining their operation. See Brostoff, "The Encyclopedist Code."

32. Holmes and Symeonides, "Representation," 1104.

33. Digest (1808), 420–21, art. 1: "Le mandat ou procuration, est un acte par lequel quelqu'un donne pouvoir à un autre, de faire pour lui et en son nom, une ou plusieurs affaires." Art. 1: "A procuration or letter of attorney is an act by which one person gives power to another to transact for him one or several affairs."

34. Holmes and Symeonides, "Representation," 1104.

35. The words "joint and several" were also employed in art. 27, p. 278.

36. This heading was not the original thought of the translators. It was lifted from William Strahan's translation of Domat. See Jean Domat, *The Civil Law*

in Its Natural Order, trans. William Strahan (Boston: Cushing, 1850), 1:463. As pointed out later in greater detail, Strahan's translation served as a "pretranslation" for a considerable portion of the digest.

37. The heading is not only heavily interpolated but also incompletely translated: the idea of "forme" is omitted in English.

38. Digest (1808), 424–25.

39. This unusual heading was drawn directly from the translation by William Strahan. "Cant" meant low or meaningless language, or (as a verb) to use language meaninglessly. Samuel Johnson advised Boswell: "Don't cant in defense of savages," and "Clear your mind of cant." See Jack Lynch, "A Guide to Eighteenth-Century English Vocabulary," April 14, 2006, http://fliphtml5.com/snac/wdff/basic. The obscure phrase "cant or auction" can be found in an English statute of 1749.

40. However, given the rudimentary training of many creole members of the bar, it is not unreasonable to think it was conceived as helpful and beneficial for them as well. See Brostoff, "The Encyclopedist Code" (describing the digest as "didactic in spirit and explanatory in style").

41. Regarding lawyers and judges generally in Spanish Louisiana, see Gilbert Din and John Harkins, *The New Orleans Cabildo: Colonial Louisiana's First City Government 1769–1803* (Baton Rouge: Louisiana State University Press, 1996), 101–17; Derek Noel Kerr, "Petty Felony, Slave Defiance and Frontier Villainy: Crime and Criminal Justice in Spanish Louisiana 1770–1803" (PhD diss., Tulane University, 1983), https://digitallibrary.tulane.edu/islandora/object/tulane:24846; Henry Dart, *Courts and Law in Colonial Louisiana* (New Orleans: Montgomery-Andree, 1921); Louis G. Kahle, "The Spanish Colonial Judiciary," *Southwestern Social Science Quarterly* 32, no. 1 (June 1951): 26–37.

42. Gaspard, "The Rise of the Louisiana Bar," 184.

43. Hans W. Baade, "Número de abogados y escribanos en la Nueva España, la provincia de Texas y la Luisiana," in *Memoria del III Congreso de historia del derecho mexicano* (Mexico City: UNAM, 1984), 119–28.

44. Kenneth Aslakson, "Immigrant Lawyers and Slavery in Territorial New Orleans," *Tulane European & Civil Law Forum* 31/32 (2017): 33. The article's appendix lists the lawyers by name, date of birth and death, time of arrival in New Orleans, point of origination, and relationship to law and slavery. Of the sixty-four lawyers in the study, Aslakson found sufficient and reliable information on only fifty-four of them.

45. At least sixteen hailed from the northeastern United States (ten from the Chesapeake region), and a few others came from the British Isles.

46. Some previous studies (including my own) crudely attempted to infer the cultural allegiance and origins of the bar by judging surnames. By that rough and somewhat speculative method, it appeared that the New Orleans bar of 1810

reflected relative parity between the two groups. Out of thirty-seven lawyers, it appeared that twenty had Creole names. Lewis William Newton, *The Americanization of French Louisiana, 1803–1860* (1929; repr., New York: Arno Press, 1980), 175; Palmer, *Mixed Jurisdictions Worldwide*, 283. In the year 1808 twenty-eight members of the bar signed a petition to the Superior Court seeking the reinstatement of Judge Workman to the bar. Fourteen signatures had Creole names, fourteen Anglo-American. [Untitled], *New York Herald*, January 25, 1809. By 1813 the balance had changed: 60 percent of the lawyers sworn in before the state supreme court were Americans, and by 1839 Americans outnumbered Creoles by a ratio of 3.5 to 1. Gaspard, "The Rise of the Louisiana Bar," 187.

47. Only 7 percent of the bar were Spanish-speaking.

48. Dargo, *Jefferson's Louisiana*, 296.

49. See generally Symeon C. Symeonides, "The Louisiana Judge: Judge, Statesman, Politician," in Palmer, *Louisiana: Microcosm*.

50. See Robert Lunn, "Exploring the Use of the Louisiana Civil Code as a Source of English Translations for Spanish Legal Terms" (master's thesis, City University, 2012), 13, https://www.academia.edu/4357269/Exploring_the_use_of_the_Louisiana_Civil_Code_as_a_source_of_English_translations_for_Spanish_legal_terms.

51. The 1825 Civil Code's final article gave a definition for thirty-five terms used in the code. See art. 3556 (1825).

52. Gaspard, "The Rise of the Louisiana Bar," 183.

53. See Warren Billings, ed., *The Historic Rules of the Supreme Court of Louisiana, 1813–1879* (Lafayette: University of Southwestern Louisiana, 1985).

54. See Acte relative à l'organisation et au système judiciaire de l'état de la Louisiane, chap. 11, arts. 240, 241 (1805): "Nul ne sera admis à exercer la profession d'avocat auprès d'aucune des Cours de cet État, s'il n'est agé de vingt-un ans accomplis, s'il n'est citoyen des États-Unis, et s'il n'a réside dans cet État, depuis au moins un an."

55. Act of the Legislature, Territory of Orleans, Regulating the Admission of Attornies at Law, March 31, 1808, chap. 30, pp. 128–38. This statute also fixed in dollar amounts the maximum legal fees that a lawyer could charge.

56. Rule of 23 November 1810, in 1 Martin (o.s.), 140 et seq. (1810).

57. Billings, *The Historic Rules*, 1–2. The rules changed frequently and somewhat later were tightened. The court's rule of November 24, 1840, required citizenship, good moral character, one year's residence, and an examination on a "Course of Studies" that included the works of Story, Vattel, the Louisiana Code, Code of Practice, the statutes of the state, the Institutes of Justinian, Domat's Civil Laws, Pothier on Obligations, Blackstone's *Commentaries*, Kent's *Commentaries*, Chitty or Bayley on bills, Starkie or Phillips on evidence, Russel on crimes, and the jurisprudence of the Louisiana Supreme Court. The burden of

examining candidates was placed on a committee of seven lawyers charged with certifying their qualifications. Ibid., 9–11.

58. Dargo, *Jefferson's Louisiana*, 261.

59. *Esquisse de la situation* (1804), 35, translated in Dargo, *Jefferson's Louisiana*, 216.

60. Nugent (unsigned) to the editor of the *Aurora, Charleston City Gazette*, February 7, 1809.

61. For example, see this traditional usage in Robert Pothier, *Traité des obligations* (Paris: Dabo Jeune, 1825), pt. 1, chap. 2, pp. 170ff., and in pt. 2, chap. 4, pp. 289ff. François-Xavier Martin followed this usage in his English translation of Pothier.

62. The phraseology "obligor and obligee" was used in some early common-law treatises and dictionaries to identify the parties who had entered into bonds. See, for example, Sir Edward Coke, *Commentary on Littleton*, 16th ed. (London: L. Hansard & Sons, 1809), vol. 2, para. 337; William Sheppard, *The Touchstone of Common Assurances* (Dublin, 1785), 368; Giles Jacob, *A New Law-Dictionary* (London: W. Strahan & W. Woodfall, 1782), s.v. "bond"; Blackstone, *Commentaries*, 2:340–41. As late as 1884 Francis Wharton stated, "Sometimes we are told of the 'obligor' and the 'obligee' of a right; and this would, perhaps, be the most satisfactory way of expressing the relationship, were it not that in English law 'obligor' and 'obligee' are terms confined to the parties to bonds" (*Commentaries on Law, Embracing Chapters on the Nature, the Source, and the History of Law* [Philadelphia: Kay & Brothers, 1884], 15).

63. The terms appear in Coke's *Commentary on Littleton*, vol. 2. In Thomas Wood, *An Institute of the Laws of England*, 3rd ed. (London, 1724), Wood states at page 288: "He that Enters into the Obligation or Bond is the Obligor, and He to whom it is made is the Obligee." See also Jacob, *A New Law-Dictionary*, s.v. "bond."

64. See the discussion in Blackstone, *Commentaries*, 2:132–35.

65. Ibid., 2:340–41. The terms appear eight times in his treatment of "an obligation."

66. The terms are translated in Gérard Cornu's *Dictionary of the Civil Code*, trans. Alain Levasseur and Marie-Eugénie Laporte-Legeais (LexisNexis, 2014), 634 as "créancier/débiteur."

67. For example, to go no further than the provisions on "obligations in solido" (chap. 4, sec. 4, pp. 278–82), the words "creditor" and "debtor" appear twenty-six and thirty-six times, respectively, in the English and French texts.

68. Justice Martin noted this mistranslation in a state supreme court opinion: "It is manifest that the word, co-obligés, is erroneously translated into co-obligees. The correct translation of this past participle is co-obligors; an obligee in English is the person in whose favor the obligation is made; an obligé in

French is the person bound to fulfil the obligation, or what we call an obligor" (Relf & Zacharie v. McDonogh, 19 La. 100 [1841]).

69. John Austin in 1832 noted the lack of development of the distinction in his day: "'Creditor' is the correlative of 'Debitor' and applies to any person who has jus in personam. The French 'Debiteur' and 'Creancier' have precisely the same meanings. The English 'Obligor' and 'Obligee' ought to bear the same signification. But in the technical language of our Law, the term 'obligation' or 'bond' has been miserably mutilated. . . . [I]t is applied exclusively to certain unilateral contracts evidenced by writing under seal" (quoted in Michael Hoeflich, *Roman and Civil Law and the Development of Anglo-American Jurisprudence in the Nineteenth Century* [Athens: University of Georgia Press, 1997], 14).

70. The 1825 redactors continued drafting in terms of the traditional language of "créancier/debiteur," but the translators now converted that systematically to "obligee/obligor."

71. See Louisiana Civil Code, art. 3556, paras. 20–21: "Obligee or Creditor.—Obligee or creditor is the person in favor of whom some obligation is contracted, whether such obligation be to pay a sum of money, or to do or not to do something." "Obligor or Debtor.—Obligor or debtor is the person who has engaged to perform some obligation."

72. See, for example, its widespread adoption in international harmonizations such as the Unidroit Principles and the uniform acts of OHADA. See Marcel Fontaine, "Position Paper on Plurality of Obligors and/or Obligees" (Unidroit, Working Group for the Preparation of Principles of International Commercial Contracts [3rd], Study L, Doc. 102, April 2007), https://nanopdf.com/download/study-l-doc-102_pdf.

73. See Succession of Barr, 219 So.2d 817 (2 Cir. Ct. App. 1969); United States v. Harang, 65 F.2d 106 (5th Cir. 1947): "The word 'profits,' therefore, in the English text of article 64 . . . is unquestionably an erroneous translation of the French word 'fruits' in the French text of the article."

74. The same translator has the peculiarity of always translating the word "animaux" (animals) as "cattle"—which is not merely a mistake but a curiosity unto itself.

75. Here we note a license often taken by the translators, which was to add extra words to the text (here the word "annuities") that have no counterpart or basis in the French text.

76. In one instance a befuddled translator translated "les fruits civils" as "civil rights" (art. 4, p. 102).

77. Succession of Barr, 219 So.2d 817.

78. See Sally Richardson, "Reframing Ameliorative Waste," Tulane Public Law Research Paper 15-15, December 2015, http://ssrn.com/abstract=2697815.

79. Blackstone, *Commentaries*, 2:122.

80. For Blackstone's treatment of "inheritance," see ibid., 2:104, 281–82. See also Sir Edward Coke, *Institutes of the Laws of England*, 7 vols. (London: E. & R. Brooke, 1794).

81. Clear seams in the translation are evident in book 2. For example, at pages 98–104 translator A's own style and signature errors are apparent; translator B then picks up at pages 104–12; translator A returns from pages 112 to 120. Translator B returns in pages 120–43.

82. The second translator made no jarring mistake of this kind. See the translation of pages 192–200 ("Of the Collation of Goods"), where "héritage" is repeatedly rendered either as "immovable" or as "tenement."

83. The origin and history of the word "cattle" suggest that the translators adopted an obsolete meaning that was once current centuries earlier. In the mid-thirteenth century, cattle meant "property," coming from Anglo-French *catel*, "property" (Old North French *catel*, Old French *chatel*), from medieval Latin *capitale*, "property, stock." Originally the word denoted movable property, especially livestock; it began to be limited to "cows and bulls" from the late sixteenth century. "Cattle," *Online Etymology Dictionary*, https://www.etymonline.com/search?q=cattle&source=ds_search. In Dr. Johnson's dictionary, the first definition given is "beasts of pasture; not wild nor domestick" (*A Dictionary of the English Language* [London: W. Strahan, 1755], s.v. "cattle"). Blackstone refers to old statutes using the term in the sense of livestock in general, as in his phrase "horses, sheep, or other cattle" (*Commentaries*, 4:243).

84. For other instances, see art. 69, p. 338, art. 73, p. 124.

85. Rodolfo Batiza, "The Louisiana Civil Code of 1808: Its Actual Sources and Present Relevance," *Tulane Law Review* 46, no. 1 (September 1971): 11.

86. Professor Batiza noted in passing the strange expression "knavish possessor," but he did not connect it to Strahan's translation (Batiza, "The Louisiana Civil Code of 1808," 30). Interestingly, Professor Dainow did not treat "knavish possessor" as an error of translation in his compiled edition, though he could hardly have failed to ponder its oddness. See annotations to arts. 3451, 3452, 3454 in Dainow, *1972 Compiled Edition*, 654–56. H. P. Nugent used the word "knavish" rather frequently in his writings, and so Strahan's word choice may not have seemed odd to him. See H. P. Nugent, *A Defence of the Honorable John Rowan and Daniel Clark, Members of Congress, against the Slanders of the Tergiversant Redacteur of the Courier* (New Orleans: Printed for the author, 1808), 24–25, 27; see also Nugent (unsigned) to the editor of the *Aurora, Charleston City Gazette*, February 7, 1809 ("making knavery to set law at defiance").

87. David Snyder, "Ancient Law and Modern Eyes," *Tulane Law Review* 69, no. 6 (June 1995): 1631; Rodolfo Batiza, "Justinian's Institute and the Louisiana Civil Code of 1808," *Tulane Law Review* 69, no. 6 (June 1995): 1639.

88. Daniel R. Coquillette, *The Civilian Writers of Doctors' Commons* (Berlin:

Duncker & Humblot, 1988), 198; Peter Stein, "The Attraction of the Civil Law in Post-Revolutionary America," *Virginia Law Review* 52, no. 3 (April 1966): 406–7.

89. The text of the Declaratory Act is set forth in Mitchell Franklin, "The Place of Thomas Jefferson in the Expulsion of Spanish Medieval Law from Louisiana," *Tulane Law Review* 16, no. 3 (April 1942): 323–26. On the reasons why Domat's authority was specifically recognized by the Declaratory Act, see John Cairns, "Spanish Law, the Teatro de la legislación universal de España e Indias, and the Background to the Drafting of the Digest of Orleans of 1808," *Tulane European & Civil Law Forum* 31/32 (2017): 108–11. On the type of legal system envisioned by the Declaratory Act, see Palmer, "Sounding the Retreat," 146–47. John Cairns argues that Domat was singled out because the legislature was influenced by his mention in Perez's *Teatro*, but an additional reason might simply be practical. What set Domat apart from other authors who might have been mentioned but were not was not only his rational arrangement and exposition of Roman law but also his accessibility in both English and French. Due to Strahan's translation, Domat's work was uniquely accessible in the vehicular languages of the Territory of Orleans.

90. No copy of the work is listed in the libraries of Livingston, Moreau-Lislet, and De Armas. Nevertheless, Mark Fernandez asserts that the translation of Domat was "almost universally used" in Louisiana, but one is not sure of the period he may be referring to, and he adduces no evidence for the claim. Warren Billings and Mark Fernandez, eds., *A Law unto Itself? Essays in the New Louisiana History* (Baton Rouge: Louisiana State University Press, 2001), 34n20.

91. Dufour v. Camfranc, 11 Mart. (o.s.) 675 (1822).

92. Coquillette, *The Civilian Writers*, 198.

93. Ibid., 206, 205.

94. Batiza, "The Louisiana Civil Code of 1808," 29.

95. On Blackstone's attraction in the United States, see Dennis R. Nolan, "Sir William Blackstone and the New Republic: A Study of Intellectual Impact," *New York University Law Review* 51, no. 5 (November 1976): 731. Edward Livingston, in defending his rights to the batture, relied upon Blackstone for the proposition that the sovereign could not take private land without the judgment of a court or a jury. Edward Livingston, *Address to the People of the United States on the Measures Pursued by the Executive with Respect to the Batture at New Orleans* (New Orleans: Bradford and Anderson, 1813).

96. The *Commentaries* were cited five times in reported opinions between 1801 and 1810 and twenty-six times between 1811 and 1820. Stephen M. Sheppard, "Legal Jambalaya," in *Re-interpreting Blackstone's "Commentaries,"* ed. Wilfrid Prest (Oxford: Hart Publishing, 2014), 102 (appendix). For civil cases, see Ronald Fonseca, "Blackstone's *Commentaries*: Foothold or Footnote in Louisiana's Antebellum Legal History" (master's thesis, University of New Orleans,

2007), 17, https://scholarworks.uno.edu/td/514/. The author's scan of the years 1809–75 showed forty-one citations to Blackstone in civil cases. According to Ronald Fonseca, Blackstone served as the Louisiana lawyer's "hornbook" for criminal law.

97. Mitchell Franklin, "Libraries of Edward Livingston and of Moreau Lislet," *Tulane Law Review* 15, no. 3 (April 1941): 406, 408.

98. An item in the newspaper reported that Blackstone's *Commentaries* had been accidentally taken out of Martin's library, and a request was made for their return. See [Untitled], *Newbern (N.C.) Herald*, September 30, 1809.

99. Michel Morin, "Blackstone and the Birth of Quebec's Distinct Legal Culture 1765–1867," in Prest, *Re-interpreting Blackstone's "Commentaries,"* 105–24.

100. John Cairns, "Blackstone in the Bayous: Inscribing Slavery in the Louisiana Digest of 1808," in Prest, *Re-interpreting Blackstone's "Commentaries,"* 88.

101. Batiza, "The Louisiana Civil Code of 1808," 25; Cairns, "Blackstone in the Bayous," 84.

102. Alejandro Guzmán Brito, "Las fuentes de las normas sobre interpretación de las leyes del 'Digest des lois civiles' ('code civil') de la Luisiana (1808/1825)," *Revista de Estudios Histórico-Jurídicos* 31 (2009): 4–5. Blackstone openly credited his civilian sources.

103. See Louis Moreau-Lislet and Henry Carleton, trans., *The Laws of "Las Siete Partidas," Which Are Still in Force in the State of Louisiana* (New Orleans: James M'Karaher, 1820), 2:1226n(a).

104. Kerr, *An Exposition*, 9.

105. Ibid., 20–26.

106. Fonseca, "Blackstone's *Commentaries*," 7 (noting Brown's references to Blackstone in briefs and arguments before the courts).

107. Quoted from Dargo, *Jefferson's Louisiana*, 115.

108. This was the first *reported* Louisiana case to cite the *Commentaries*. Territory v. Nugent, 1 Mart. (o.s.) 42 (1810), 1 Mart. (o.s.) 108, and 1 Mart. (o.s.) 169.

109. "The Memorial of H. P. Nugent," January 20, 1809, 75; see also "A Letter to the Gentlemen of the Petit-Jury, in the Trial of the Action, Nugent vs. Garland," June 1, 1808, which is found among the assorted documents in Nugent, *A Letter to His Excellency*, 35. See further cites to Blackstone, *Commentaries*, on pages 5 (on duels) and 7 (on libel). There are further citations to Blackstone in Nugent's defense of Pierre Dormenon on page 110.

110. Blackstone, *Commentaries*, 110.

111. Nugent, *An Account of the Proceedings*, 40.

112. Territory v. Nugent, 1 Mart. (o.s.) 169 (1810). Incidentally, Lewis Kerr (*An Exposition*, 114) pointed out that Blackstone's statement concerning the immateriality of truth as a defense to criminal libel (Blackstone, *Commentaries*, 3:125–26) was questionable. Kerr thought that the maxim "the greater the truth the

greater the libel" was contradicted by some authorities and "probably is not the law."

113. The source passages appear in Blackstone, *Commentaries*, 1:69, 71.

114. See Batiza, "The Louisiana Civil Code of 1808"; Cairns, "Blackstone in the Bayous"; and Thomas W. Tucker, "Sources of Louisiana's Law of Persons: Blackstone, Domat and the French Codes," *Tulane Law Review* 44, no. 2 (February 1970): 264–95.

115. The remaining fragment and its turbulent syntax are as follows: "When a thing has been formed by a mixture of several materials belonging to different proprietors, each of which cannot be considered as the principal substance, the person unknown to whom the materials have been mixed may require the division of the same."

116. A serious omission occurs in art. 230, p. 202, where the translation skips a line.

117. See, inter alia, the following interpolations without textual basis: art. 53, p. 332 (adding the phrase "and which were alienated by her husband"); art. 34, p. 84 (adding "or assignees"); art. 50, p. 354 (adding "or claims"); art. 79, p. 72 (adding "above the age of puberty"); art. 26, p. 434 (adding "as qualifying a person to become a legal surety"); art. 97, p. 278 (adding "or joint and several"); art. 203, p. 252 (adding "[between the living]"); art. 145, p. 240 (adding "possession"); art. 103, p. 230 (adding "or codicil"); art. 10, p. 210 (adding "open" concubinage); art. 3, p. 208 (adding "[in prospect of death]"); art. 2, p. 208 (adding "[between living persons]"); art. 223, p. 200 (adding "among themselves"); art. 209, p. 196 (adding "order to"); art. 5, p. 146 (adding "the institution of heir, contained in"); art. 206, p. 302 (adding "[can not be relieved against his engagements]").

118. See English arts. 193 and 194, p. 192, and compare with French arts. 193 and 194, p. 193. Note also that the French word *rapport* is translated as "collation" generally in this section, though in art. 193 it is anomalously rendered "collect."

BIBLIOGRAPHY

Aslakson, Kenneth. "Immigrant Lawyers and Slavery in Territorial New Orleans." *Tulane European & Civil Law Forum* 31/32 (2017): 33–77.

Baade, Hans W. "Número de abogados y escribanos en la Nueva España, la provincia de Texas y la Luisiana." In *Memoria del III Congreso de historia del derecho mexicano*. Mexico City: UNAM, 1984.

Bailey, Richard W. "The Foundation of English in the Louisiana Purchase: New Orleans, 1800–1850." *American Speech* 78 (2003): 363–84.

Batiza, Rodolfo. "Justinian's Institute and the Louisiana Civil Code of 1808." *Tulane Law Review* 69, no. 6 (June 1995): 1639–48.

———. "The Louisiana Civil Code of 1808: Its Actual Sources and Present Relevance." *Tulane Law Review* 46, no. 1 (September 1971): 4–165.

———. "Origins of Modern Codification of the Civil Law: The French Experience and Its Implications for Louisiana Law." *Tulane Law Review* 56, no. 2 (February 1982): 477–601.

Billings, Warren, ed. *The Historic Rules of the Supreme Court of Louisiana, 1813–1879*. Lafayette: University of Southwestern Louisiana, 1985.

———. "A Judicial Legacy: The Last Will and Testament of François-Xavier Martin." *Louisiana History: The Journal of the Louisiana Historical Association* 25 (1984): 277–89.

Billings, Warren, and Mark Fernandez, eds. *A Law unto Itself? Essays in the New Louisiana History*. Baton Rouge: Louisiana State University Press, 2001.

Blackstone, William. *Commentaries on the Laws of England*. 4 vols. Chicago: University of Chicago Press, 1979.

Bradley, Jared W. *Interim Appointment: W. C. C. Claiborne Letter Book, 1804–1805*. Baton Rouge: Louisiana State University Press, 2002.

Brostoff, Seth. "The Encyclopedist Code: *Ancien Droit* French Legal Encyclopedias and Their Verbatim Influence on the Louisiana Digest of 1808." *Journal of Civil Law Studies* 13 (forthcoming).

Brown, Elizabeth Gaspar. "Legal Systems in Conflict: Orleans Territory, 1804–1812." *American Journal of Legal History* 1, no. 1 (January 1957): 35–75.

Cairns, John. "Blackstone in the Bayous: Inscribing Slavery in the Louisiana Digest of 1808." In *Re-interpreting Blackstone's "Commentaries,"* edited by Wilfrid Prest, 73–94. Oxford: Hart Publishing, 2014.

———. *Codification, Transplants, and History: Law Reform in Louisiana (1808) and Quebec (1866)*. Clarke, N.J.: Talbot, 2015.

———. "Spanish Law, the Teatro de la legislación universal de España e Indias, and the Background to the Drafting of the Digest of Orleans of 1808." *Tulane European & Civil Law Forum* 31/32 (2017): 79–120.

Carlisle, Aimee Jeanne. "Language Attrition in Louisiana Creole French." Honors thesis, University of California, Davis, 2010. https://www.yumpu.com/en/document/view/38092426/language-attrition-in-louisiana-creole-french.

Chiorazzi, Michael. "François-Xavier Martin: Printer, Lawyer, Jurist." *Duke Law Magazine* 7, no. 1 (Winter 1989).

Claiborne, William C. C. *Official Letter Books of W. C. C. Claiborne, 1801–1816.* Vol. 4. Edited by Dunbar Rowland. Jackson, Miss.: State Department of History and Archives, 1917.

Coke, Sir Edward. *Commentary on Littleton*. Vol. 2. 16th ed. London: L. Hansard & Sons, 1809.

———. *Institutes of the Laws of England*. 7 vols. London: E. & R. Brooke, 1794.

Coquillette, Daniel R. *The Civilian Writers of Doctors' Commons*. Berlin: Duncker & Humblot, 1988.

Cornu, Gérard. *Dictionary of the Civil Code*. Translated by Alain Levasseur and Marie-Eugénie Laporte-Legeais. LexisNexis, 2014.

Dainow, Joseph, ed. *1972 Compiled Edition of the Civil Codes of Louisiana*. Vol. 17. St. Paul, Minn.: West, 1973.

Dargo, George. *Colony to Empire: Episodes in American Legal History*. Clark, N.J.: Lawbook Exchange, 2011.

———. *Jefferson's Louisiana: Politics and the Clash of Legal Traditions*. Revised edition. Clark, N.J.: Lawbook Exchange, 2009. First published in 1975.

Dart, Henry. *Courts and Law in Colonial Louisiana*. New Orleans: Montgomery-Andree, 1921.

Davis, William C. *The Pirates Laffite: The Treacherous World of the Corsairs of the Gulf*. Orlando: Harcourt, 2005.

Debien, Gabriel, and René LeGardeur. "Les colons de Saint-Domingue réfugiés á la Louisiane (1792–1804)." *Revue de la Louisiane* 10, no. 2 (Winter 1981): 97–141.

Degges, Dan. "The Mexican Association: The Secret Society behind the Aaron Burr Conspiracy." Unpublished manuscript, University of Arkansas at Monticello. www.academia.edu/4358596/The_Mexican_Association.

Dessens, Nathalie. "The Sounds of Babel: Staging American Ethnic Diversity in Early Nineteenth-Century New Orleans." Special issue, *Complutense Journal of English Studies* 23 (2015): 15–27.

Din, Gilbert, and John Harkins. *The New Orleans Cabildo: Colonial Louisiana's First City Government, 1769–1803*. Baton Rouge: Louisiana State University Press, 1996.

Domat, Jean. *The Civil Law in Its Natural Order*. Vol. 1. Translated by William Strahan. Boston: Cushing, 1850. Originally published in 1722.

Dubuisson, Edward B. "The Codes of Louisiana (Originals Written in French; Errors of Translation)." In *Report of the Louisiana Bar Association, Vol. 25, for 1924*, 143–55. New Orleans: Montgomery-Andree Printing Co., 1924.

———. "Errors of Translation in the Codes." *Loyola Law Journal* 5, no. 3 (May 1924): 163–76.

Earl, John L., III. "Talleyrand in Philadelphia." *Pennsylvania Magazine of History and Biography* 91 (1967): 282–98.

"Extract of a Letter from a Gentleman in New Orleans, Dated September 17, 1807." *Political Observatory* (Walpole, N.H.), September 17, 1807.

Faber, Eberhard. *Building the Land of Dreams: New Orleans and the Transformation of Early America*. Princeton, N.J.: Princeton University Press, 2016.

Fernandez, Marc. *From Chaos to Continuity*. Baton Rouge: Louisiana State University Press, 2001.

Fonseca, Ronald. "Blackstone's *Commentaries*: Foothold or Footnote in Louisiana's Antebellum Legal History." Master's thesis, University of New Orleans, 2007. https://scholarworks.uno.edu/td/514/.

Fontaine, Marcel. "Position Paper on Plurality of Obligors and/or Obligees." Unidroit, Working Group for the Preparation of Principles of International Commercial Contracts (3rd). Study L, Doc. 102, April 2007. https://nanopdf.com/download/study-l-doc-102_pdf.

Foote, Henry Stuart. *The Bench and Bar of the South and Southwest*. New York, 1876.

Franklin, Marc. "The Origins and Constitutionality of Limitations on Truth as a Defense in Tort Law." *Stanford Law Review* 16, no. 4 (1964): 789–848.

Franklin, Mitchell. "Libraries of Edward Livingston and of Moreau Lislet." *Tulane Law Review* 15, no. 3 (April 1941): 401–14.

———. "The Place of Thomas Jefferson in the Expulsion of Spanish Medieval Law from Louisiana." *Tulane Law Review* 16, no. 3 (April 1942): 319–38.

———. "Some Observations on the Influence of French Law on the Early Civil Codes of Louisiana." In *Le Droit civil français: Livre-souvenir des journées du droit civil français*. Paris: Le Barreau de Montréal, 1936.

Gaspard, Elizabeth. "The Rise of the Louisiana Bar: The Early Period, 1813–1839." *Louisiana History* 28, no. 2 (Spring 1987): 183–97.

Gayarré, Charles. *History of Louisiana*. Vol. 4, *The American Domination*. New Orleans: Gresham Publishing Co., 1879.

Greiner, Meinrad. *The Louisiana Digest (1804–1841)*. New Orleans: Benjamin Levy, 1841.

Guyot, J.-N. *Répertoire universel et raisonné de jurisprudence civile, criminelle, canonique et bénéficiale*. 64 vols. Paris, 1775–83.

Guzmán Brito, Alejandro. "Las fuentes de las normas sobre interpretación de las leyes del 'Digest des lois civiles' ('code civil') de la Luisiana (1808/1825)." *Revista de Estudios Histórico-Jurídicos* 31 (2009): 4–5.

Hoeflich, Michael. *Roman and Civil Law and the Development of Anglo-American Jurisprudence in the Nineteenth Century.* Athens: University of Georgia Press, 1997.

Holmes, Wendell H., and Symeon C. Symeonides. "Representation, Mandate and Agency: A Kommentar on Louisiana's New Law." *Tulane Law Review* 73, no. 4 (March 1999): 1087–1159.

Hood, John T., Jr. "History and Development of the Louisiana Civil Code." *Louisiana Law Review* 19, no. 1 (1958): 18–33.

Hunt, Charles Havens. *Life of Edward Livingston.* New York: Appleton & Co., 1864.

Hunt, Louise Livingston. *Memoir of Mrs. Edward Livingston.* New York, 1886.

Jacob, Giles. *A New Law-Dictionary.* London: W. Strahan & W. Woodfall, 1782.

Johnson, Erica Robin. "Louisiana Identity on Trial: The Superior Court Case of Pierre Benonime Dormenon." Master's thesis, University of Texas at Arlington, 2007. https://rc.library.uta.edu/uta-ir/bitstream/handle/10106/622/umi-uta-1842.pdf?sequence=1&isAllowed=y.

Johnson, Samuel. *A Dictionary of the English Language.* London: W. Strahan, 1755.

Jones, H. G. "Martin, François-Xavier." In *Dictionary of North Carolina Biography*, edited by William S. Powell, vol. 4, L–O, 224–25. Chapel Hill: University of North Carolina Press, 1991.

Kahle, Louis G. "The Spanish Colonial Judiciary." *Southwestern Social Science Quarterly* 32, no. 1 (June 1951): 26–37.

Kerr, Derek Noel. "Petty Felony, Slave Defiance and Frontier Villainy: Crime and Criminal Justice in Spanish Louisiana 1770–1803." PhD diss., Tulane University, 1983. https://digitallibrary.tulane.edu/islandora/object/tulane:24846.

Kerr, Lewis. *An Exposition of the Criminal Laws of the Territory.* New Orleans: Bradford & Anderson, 1806.

Keyes, Pamela. "Auguste Davezac, the Creole Celebrity That History Forgot." *Historia Obscura*, October 2, 2018. https://www.historiaobscura.com/auguste-davezac-the-creole-celebrity-that-history-forgot/.

Klinger, Thomas A. "Language Labels and Language Use among Cajuns and Creoles in Louisiana." University of Pennsylvania Working Papers in Linguistics, vol. 9, no. 2, 2003. https://repository.upenn.edu/cgi/viewcontent.cgi?article=1454&context=pwpl.

Lachance, Paul. "The Foreign French." In *Creole New Orleans*, edited by Arnold R. Hirsch and Joseph Logsdon, 101–30. Baton Rouge: Louisiana State University Press, 1992.

Lafon, Bernard. *Annuaire louisianais pour l'année 1809*. New Orleans: Lafon, 1808.

———. *Calendrier de commerce de la Nouvelle-Orléans pour l'Année 1807 (J. Renard 1806)*. New Orleans: Lafon, 1807.

Lebreton, Marietta Marie. "A History of the Territory of Orleans, 1803–1812." PhD diss., Louisiana State University, 1969. LSU Historical Dissertations and Theses 1554.

"Letter of October 7th, 1808." In *Territorial Papers of the United States*, edited by Clarence Carter, 9:802. Washington, D.C.: United States Government Printing Office, 1940.

Livingston, Edward. *Address to the People of the United States on the Measures Pursued by the Executive with Respect to the Batture at New Orleans*. New Orleans: Bradford and Anderson, 1813.

Lunn, Robert. "Exploring the Use of the Louisiana Civil Code as a Source of English Translations for Spanish Legal Terms." Master's thesis, City University, 2012. https://www.academia.edu/4357269/Exploring_the_use_of_the_Louisiana_Civil_Code_as_a_source_of_English_translations_for_Spanish_legal_terms.

Lynch, Jack. "A Guide to Eighteenth-Century English Vocabulary." April 14, 2006. http://fliphtml5.com/snac/wdff/basic.

"Major Davezac." *United States Magazine and Democratic Review* 16 (1845): 109–10.

Martin, F.-X. *The History of Louisiana: From the Earliest Period*. 2 vols. New Orleans: Lyman and Beardslee, 1827.

Maurel, Blanche. "Une Société de pensée à Saint-Domingue, le 'Cercle des Philadelphes' au Cap-Français." *Revue française d'histoire d'outre-Mer* 48 (1961): 234–66.

McAuley, Michael. "The Pedagogical Code." *Louisiana Law Review* 63, no. 4 (Summer 2003): 1293–1304.

Moreau-Lislet, Louis, and Henry Carleton, trans. *The Laws of "Las Siete Partidas," Which Are Still in Force in the State of Louisiana*. Vol. 2. New Orleans: James M'Karaher, 1820.

Moréteau, Olivier. "François-Xavier Martin Revisited." *Louisiana Bar Journal* 60, no. 6 (2013): 474–79.

Morin, Michel. "Blackstone and the Birth of Quebec's Distinct Legal Culture 1765–1867." In *Re-interpreting Blackstone's "Commentaries,"* edited by Wilfrid Prest, 105–24. Oxford: Hart Publishing, 2014.

Newton, Lewis William. *The Americanization of French Louisiana, 1803–1860*. New York: Arno Press, 1980. First published in 1929.

Noble, Stuart Grayson. "Governor Claiborne and the Public School System of the Territorial Government of Louisiana." *Louisiana Historical Quarterly* 11, no. 4 (October 1928): 535–52.

———. "Schools of New Orleans during the First Quarter of the Nineteenth Century." *Louisiana Historical Quarterly* 14, no. 1 (January 1931): 65–78.
Nolan, Dennis R. "Sir William Blackstone and the New Republic: A Study of Intellectual Impact." *New York University Law Review* 51, no. 5 (November 1976): 731–68.
Nolte, Vincent. *Fifty Years in Both Hemispheres; or, Reminiscences of a Merchant's Life*. London: Redfield, 1854.
Nugent, H. P. *An Account of the Proceedings Had in the Superior Court of the Territory of Orleans, Against Thierry and Nugent for Libels and Contempt of Court, with an Account of Nugent's Trial on an Indictment for a Libel*. Philadelphia, 1810.
———. *A Caution to gentlemen who use Sheridan's dictionary: To which are added, for the assistance of foreigners and natives, select rules for pronouncing English with precision and elegance*. 3rd ed. London: G. Bourne and T. Turner, 1790. Reprinted 3rd ed. Cork: J. Sullivan, 1791.
———. *Collection of the Heroic & Civic Actions of the French Republicans*. Philadelphia, 1794.
———. *Defence of A. Davezac de Castras, Esq., Counsellor at Law, Now Absent, Against the Calumnies of F. X. Martin, One of the Judges of the Superior Court of the Territory of Orleans*. New Orleans, 1811.
———. *A Defence of the Honorable John Rowan and Daniel Clark, Members of Congress, against the Slanders of the Tergiversant Redacteur of the Courier*. New Orleans: Printed for the author, 1808.
———. "Gulliver's Account of the Grand Academy of Projectors at Lagado."
———. *H. P. Nugent's Reply to the Calumnies of the Honorable F. X. Martin, One of the Judges of the Superior Court of the Territory of Orleans*. Natchez, [Miss.], 1811.
———. *Letter from His Sapient Majesty Our Sovereign Lord King Solomon, Chancellor of the Lost Will and Testament of the God Who "Bequeathed" to Us the Ocean*. New Orleans, 1809.
———. *A Letter to His Excellency William C. C. Claiborne, Governor of the Territory of Orleans*. New Orleans, 1808.
———. *Mr. Nugent's Vindication of His Writings, in a Letter to Mr. Lilly*. Albany, 1799.
———. *Observations on the Trial of Peter Dormenon, Esquire*. New Orleans: Printed for the author, 1809.
———. *A Philippic against the Calumniator of the Immortal Washington*. Charleston: Thomas Bowen, 1801.
Onofrio, Jan. "D'Avezac, Auguste Geneviève Valentin." In *Louisiana Biographical Dictionary*, 72–73. St. Clair Shores, Mich.: Somerset Publishers, 1999.
Ostroukh, Asya. "The Mystery of the *Mixité* around the Title of the Louisiana Digest of the Civil Laws of 1808." *Loyola Law Review* 62 (2016): 725–48.

Palmer, Vernon Valentine, ed. *Louisiana: Microcosm of a Mixed Jurisdiction.* Durham, N.C.: Carolina Academic Press, 1999.

———. *The Louisiana Civilian Experience: Critiques of Codification in a Mixed Jurisdiction.* Durham, N.C.: Carolina Academic Press, 2005.

———. "The Man behind the de la Vergne Volume." Paper presented at the conference "A Celebration of the Civil Law," Tulane University Law School, November 6, 2019.

———, ed. *Mixed Jurisdictions Worldwide: The Third Legal Family.* 2nd ed. Cambridge: Cambridge University Press, 2012.

———. "The Quest to Implant Civilian Method in Louisiana: Tracing the Origins of Judicial Methodology (the Tucker Lecture)." *Louisiana Law Review* 73, no. 3 (2013): 793–819.

———. "Sounding the Retreat: The Exit of Spanish Law in Early Louisiana." *Tulane European & Civil Law Forum* 31/32 (2017): 121–56.

———. "The Strange Science of Codifying Slavery: Moreau Lislet and the Louisiana Digest of 1808." *Tulane European & Civil Law Forum* 24 (2009): 83–113.

Pascal, Robert. "Of the Civil Code and Us." In *Robert Anthony Pascal: A Priest of Right Order*, edited by Olivier Moréteau, 1–24. Baton Rouge: Claitor's, 2010.

———. "Sources of the Digest of 1808: A Reply to Professor Batiza." *Tulane Law Review* 46, no. 4 (April 1972): 603–27.

Pothier, Robert. *Traité des obligations.* Paris: Dabo Jeune, 1825.

———. *A Treatise on Obligations.* 2 vols. Newbern, N.C.: Martin & Ogden, 1802.

Prest, Wilfrid, ed. *Re-interpreting Blackstone's "Commentaries."* Oxford: Hart Publishing, 2014.

Richardson, Sally. "Reframing Ameliorative Waste." Tulane Public Law Research Paper 15-15, December 2015. http://ssrn.com/abstract=2697815.

Riley, Martin L. "The Development of Education in Louisiana prior to Statehood." *Louisiana Historical Quarterly* 19 (July 1936): 622–24.

Saint-André, Jean-Bon. *A Summary Journal of the Cruise Undertaken for the Purpose of Protecting the Chesapeake Convoy, by the Fleet of the French Republic.* Philadelphia: Benjamin Franklin Bache, 1794.

Scharf, J. T., and Thompson Westcott. *History of Philadelphia 1609–1884.* Vol. 2. Philadelphia, 1884.

Scott, Rebecca. "Paper Thin: Freedom and Re-enslavement in the Diaspora of the Haitian Revolution." *Law and History Review* 29 (2011): 1031–60.

Sheppard, Stephen M. "Legal Jambalaya." In *Re-interpreting Blackstone's "Commentaries,"* edited by Wilfrid Prest, 95–104. Oxford: Hart Publishing, 2014.

Sheppard, William. *The Touchstone of Common Assurances.* Dublin, 1785.

Snyder, David. "Ancient Law and Modern Eyes." *Tulane Law Review* 69, no. 6 (June 1995): 1631–38.

Stein, Peter. "The Attraction of the Civil Law in Post-Revolutionary America." *Virginia Law Review* 52, no. 3 (April 1966): 403–34.
Suarez, Raleigh A. "Chronicle of a Failure: Public Education in Antebellum Louisiana." *Louisiana History: The Journal of the Louisiana Historical Association* 12, no. 2 (Spring 1971): 109–22.
Symeonides, Symeon C. "The Louisiana Judge: Judge, Statesman, Politician." In *Louisiana: Microcosm of a Mixed Jurisdiction*, edited by Vernon V. Palmer, 89–103. Durham, N.C.: Carolina Academic Press, 1999.
Thomas, LaVerne, III. *LeDoux: A Pioneer Franco-American Family*. New Orleans: Polyanthos, 1982.
Tucker, Thomas W. "Sources of Louisiana's Law of Persons: Blackstone, Domat and the French Codes." *Tulane Law Review* 44, no. 2 (February 1970): 264–95.
Vogel, Robert. "*Historical Memoir of the War in West Florida and Louisiana in 1814–1815, with an Atlas.*" Book review. *Louisiana History* 42, no. 1 (Winter 2001): 113–15.
Walker, Alexander. *The Life of Andrew Jackson*. New York: Derby & Jackson, 1859.
Ward, Roger K. "The Death of the French Language in Louisiana Law." In *Louisiana: Microcosm of a Mixed Jurisdiction*, edited by Vernon V. Palmer, 41–60. Durham, N.C.: Carolina Academic Press, 1999.
———. "The French Language in Louisiana Law and Legal Education: A Requiem." *Louisiana Law Review* 57, no. 4 (Summer 1997): 1283–1324.
Wharton, Francis. *Commentaries on Law, Embracing Chapters on the Nature, the Source, and the History of Law*. Philadelphia: Kay & Brothers, 1884.
Wood, Thomas. *An Institute of the Laws of England*. 3rd ed. London, 1724.
Young, Janice Deitch. *The Barrosse and Davezac Families*. Metairie, La.: Private publication, 2002.

INDEX

Acadians, 25
Adet, Pierre-Auguste, 22
alcaldes ordinarios, 57
anglicized translation, 59
anglophone population, 28, 46, 52–53, 55–59, 68, 74, 78, 82, 119
Aslakson, Kenneth, 58
Austin, John, 63

Baade, Hans, 57–58
Batiza, Rodolfo, 49–52, 70–71, 75–76, 78, 124; debate with David Snyder, 73–74
Battle of New Orleans, 15, 36, 43
batture controversy, 15, 17, 18, 29, 30, 107, 111, 125
Black Code, 28
Blackstone, Sir William, 8, 32, 49, 51–52, 61, 66, 68, 75–78, 89, 94, 103, 118, 121, 124, 126
Blanque, Jean, 11, 18, 103
Boré, Étienne de, 28, 104
Bradford, James, 5, 30
Brito, Alejandro Guzmán, 76
Brown, James, 1, 5, 17–19, 28, 49, 77, 107
Burr, Aaron, 18, 30, 107, 130

Cairns, John, 76, 78, 125
Cajun French, 25, 110
Carleton, Henry, 42
Cenas, Blaise, 30–31, 85, 91, 101, 102, 112
Civil Code "oversight committee," 11, 50, 104
Claiborne, Gov. William Charles Cole, 7, 10, 15, 17–19, 31, 46, 69, 105–7
Code Napoléon, 1, 49–50
Collège d'Orléans, 20, 36–38, 41, 116n7

Constitution of 1812, 26
contempt power, judicial use of, 5–7
Coquillette, Daniel, 75
Creole French, 24–26, 109–10, 120–21, 130, 132
Crimes Act of 1805, 28

Dainow, Joseph, 47–48, 79
Dargo, George, 10, 52, 58, 60, 117
Davezac, Auguste de Castera, 2–3, 5, 6, 14–15; diplomatic career of, 43; legal reputation of, 42–44; life of, 40–45; political career of, 43–44; relation to Jackson, 17, 43; relation to Lafittes, 42; relation to Livingston, 6, 17; as translator at Superior Court, 15. *See also* Nugent/Davezac translation of the Digest of Orleans
Davezac, Jules, 17, 40, 41
Davezac, Louise (wife of Livingston), 6, 14, 40, 102
Declaratory Act of 1806, 74
de la Vergne volume, 49
Derbigny, Pierre, 43, 60
"didactic" bilingualism, 55
Digest of Orleans. *See* Nugent/Davezac translation of the Digest of Orleans
Domat, Jean, 49–53, 70–75, 121, 125
Dormenon, Judge Pierre, 5, 7–8, 16, 30–31, 38–39, 95, 103, 106, 116, 126, 132, 134
Dubuisson, Edward, 47

Esneault, Judge Louis, 38
exposé des motifs, absence of drafters', 49

Febrero Adicionado, 49, 53
Foote, Henry Stuart, 44
Francophone lawyers, 26, 56, 58
Franklin, Mitchell, 55

Gaspard, Elizabeth, 57
Genêt, Edmond-Charles, 22, 108n6
Grymes, Attorney-General Philip, 8, 101–2
Guzmán Brito, Alejandro, 76

"high language," English as: in commerce, 26; in legal affairs, 26–27
Holmes, Andrew Hunter, 5, 8, 93
Holmes, Wendell, 55–56
Hughes, John, 49–50, 87, 104
Hunt, Charles Haves, 41–42

in solido liability, 56, 63, 122

Jackson, President Andrew, 15, 36–37, 41, 43
Johnson, Erica, 31

Kerr, Lewis, 18, 28, 30, 76, 83, 102, 104, 126

Lafon, Bernard, 13
La Laterne magique, 26, 50
Lancasterian system of education, 36
Las siete partidas, 42, 63, 76, 126, 133
Latour, Arsène LaCarrière, 16, 36–37
Le Courrier de la Louisiane, 4–5, 26
Le Moniteur de la Louisiane, 26, 31, 112
Le Télégraphe, 7, 26, 29, 111
Lewis, Judge Joshua, 4, 42; Bayou Bridge case, 7, 91, 102; disbarment of Workman and Dormenon, 7–8; and Nugent libel trial, 4, 6–9, 30–31, 33–35, 85–87
libel, truth not a defense against, 8
Livingston, Edward, 5–6, 11, 14–15, 17, 18, 28–29, 40, 42, 43, 45, 49, 60, 107, 115–16, 125–26, 131–32
Louisiana lawyers and judges, 27–28, 58–60

Martin, Judge François-Xavier, 58; Blackstone's influence on, 78; *History of Louisiana*, 27; and Nugent's trial, 4–9, 85–94; satirized by Nugent, 32–35; as translator of Pothier, 6
Mather, Mayor James, 31
Mathews, George, 58–59
Mazureau, Étienne, 5
Mexican Association, 18
Moreau-Lislet, Louis, 5, 8, 17, 19, 28, 42, 43, 63, 78, 126
Moreau de Saint-Mery, Médéric Louis Elie, 35

New Orleans: bilingual newspapers in, 26; census of 1806, 24; educational system, absence of, 25; and immigration from St. Domingue, 25; multilingualism in, 24–25; and translations, dependence on, 27
Nolte, Vincent, 5, 40, 42, 105
Nugent, Henry Paul, 2–3, 6–7, 10–11, 60; arrival and life in United States, 14, 15–16, 20–24; *A Caution to Gentlemen Who Use Sheridan's Dictionary*, 21; *Collection of the Heroic & Civic Actions of the French Republicans*, 22; command of English and use of "code words," 31; defense of free press, 85–94; as editor of *Le Télégraphe*, 29; education of, 20–21; on education in New Orleans, 25; pardoned by Claiborne, 19, 31; at Pointe Coupée 38–39; as professor of English language, Collège d'Orléans, 36; as proprietor of language school in New Orleans, 28; and regents of

the Collège d'Orléans, clash with, 37–38; relation with Sheridan, 21; satires of Judge Martin, 7, 32–35; translation of LaCarrière Latour's book, 16, 36, 37; as translator at Superior Court, 15; trial for libel, 4, 6–9, 30–31, 33–35, 85–87

Nugent/Davezac translation of the Digest of Orleans: background influence of Blackstone on, 52, 75–78; Claiborne's negative view of, 10, 46; confusion over certain civilian concepts, 64–66, 66–68; and French-preference rule, 47; legal status of English text, 47; and Pascal/Batiza debate, relevance to, 49, 51; pedagogic undercurrent of, 55–57; and Strahan translation, indebtedness to, 70–75; translators' compensation for, 12

obligor/obligee distinction, 61–64
Onofrio, Jan, 44–45
Orleans Gazette, 5, 30, 101, 103–5, 107, 111

Pascal, Robert, 49, 52, 76
Pichon, Louis-André, 22
Plantation-Society French (Colonial French), 25
Pointe Coupée Parish, 5, 18, 38–39
Polk, President James, Davezac campaigns for, 43–44
Porter, Alexander, 59
Pothier, Robert Joseph: as legal source for drafters, 51, 53; Martin's translation of treatise, 6, 32–33, 101
Poydras, Julien, as president of the Legislative Council, 5, 11–12, 18, 38–39
Practice Act of 1805, 28
Projet du Gouvernement (1800), 49, 50, 51
Provosty, Dr. Auguste, 39

Richardson, Sally, 65–66
Ruotte, Antoine-Étienne, 35
Ruotte, Josephine, 35–36, 39, 113

Saint-Domingue, 6, 8, 14, 16, 25, 35, 40–41, 109, 113, 130, 133
Sala Capitular, 4
Sheridan, Thomas, 21, 108
Snyder, David, debate with Rodolfo Batiza, 73–74
Standard French, 109–10
Strahan, William, 70–75, 82, 119–20, 124–25
Strahan translation of Domat, 70–74
Symeonides, Symeon, 55–56

Talleyrand-Périgord, Charles-Maurice de, 22, 108
territorial legislature, 1, 74, 107
Territory v. Nugent (1810), 6, 77, 78, 112
Thierry, J. B. S., 4–5, 33, 85, 94, 101, 134
Tucker, Thomas, 78

Ward, Roger, 47
Wilkinson, Gen. James, 30
Workman, James, 7, 18, 27–28, 30, 39, 83, 86, 95

Young, Janet Deitch, 42

Zenger, John Peter, 7, 35

www.ingramcontent.com/pod-product-compliance
Lightning Source LLC
Chambersburg PA
CBHW031322160426
43196CB00007B/621